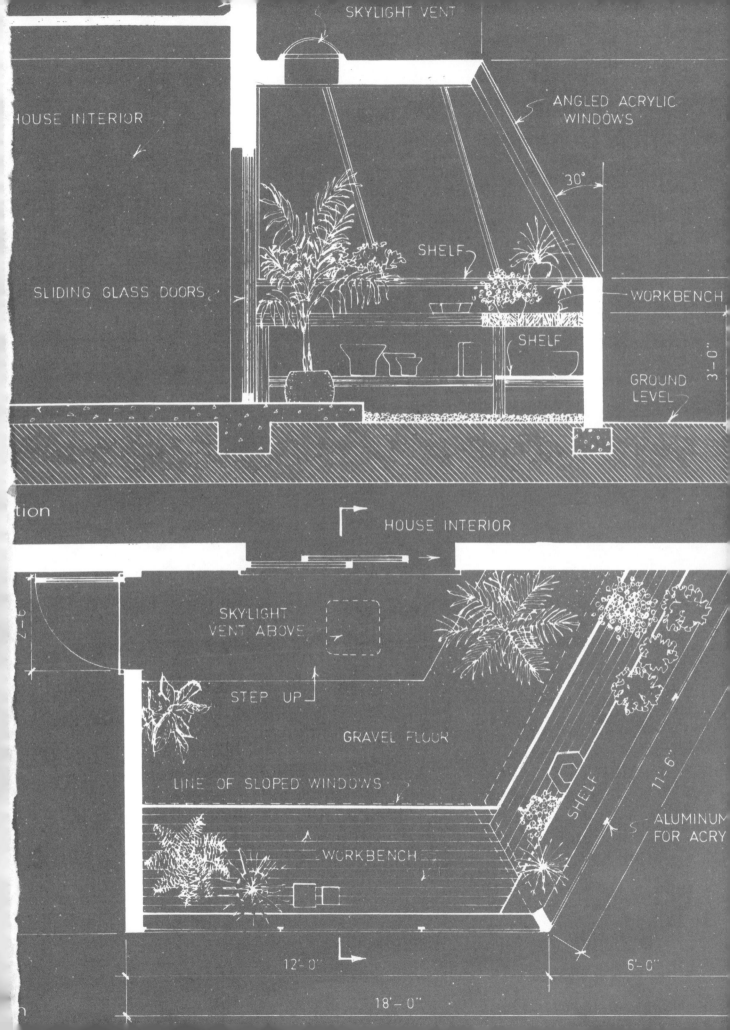

SKYLIGHT VENT

HOUSE INTERIOR

ANGLED ACRYLIC
WINDOWS

30°

SHELF

SLIDING GLASS DOORS

WORKBENCH

SHELF

GROUND
LEVEL

3'-0"

tion

HOUSE INTERIOR

SKYLIGHT
VENT ABOVE

STEP UP

GRAVEL FLOOR

11'-6"

LINE OF SLOPED WINDOWS

SHELF

WORKBENCH

ALUMINUM
FOR ACRY

12'-0"

6'-0"

18'-0"

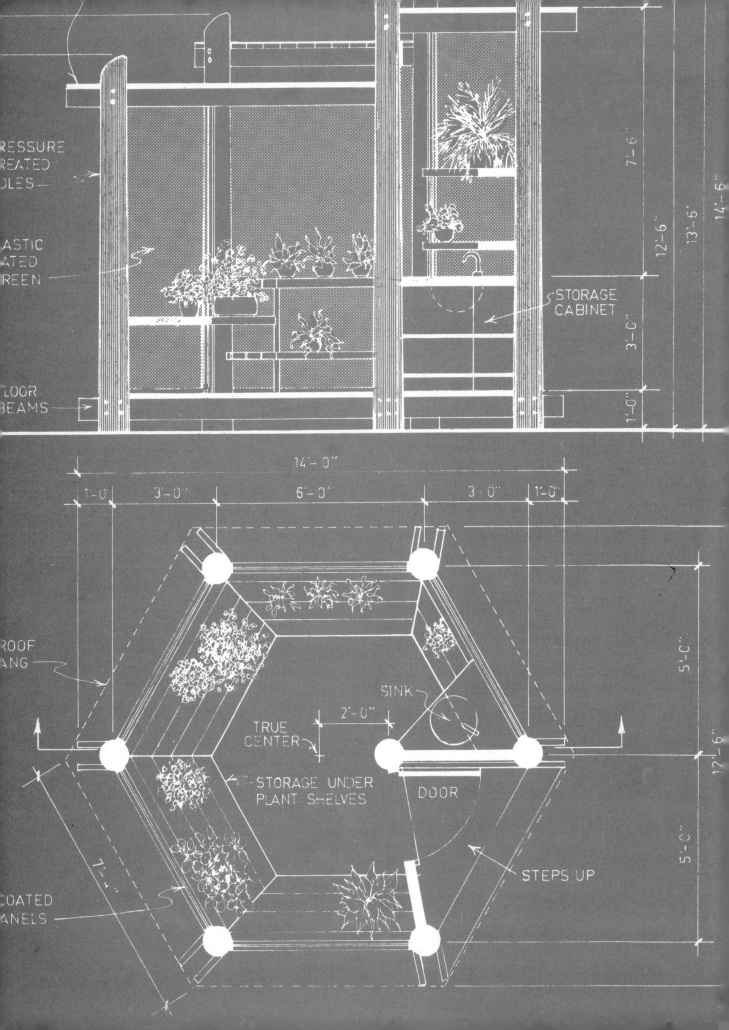

PRESSURE
TREATED
POLES

PLASTIC
COATED
SCREEN

FLOOR
BEAMS

7'-6"

12'-6"

13'-6"

14'-6"

STORAGE
CABINET

3'-0"

1'-0"

14'-0"

1'-0"   3'-0"   6'-0"   3'-0"   1'-0"

ROOF
OVERHANG

TRUE
CENTER

2'-0"

SINK

STORAGE UNDER
PLANT SHELVES

DOOR

STEPS UP

COATED
PANELS

5'-0"

12'-6"

5'-0"

7'-

your homemade greenhouse

and how to build it

by Jack Kramer

WALKER AND COMPANY

NEW YORK

Cover Credits

*Color photos by Clark Photo/Graphic, blueprint
drawing by Adrian Martinez, and B&W photo
of window greenhouse by Max Eckart, Paul
DuPont, Designer.*

First published in the United States of America in
1975 by the Walker Publishing Company, Inc.
Published simultaneously in Canada by Fitzhenry &
Whiteside, Limited, Toronto
ISBN: 0-8027-0495-6
Library of Congress Catalog Card Number:
74-31926
Lithographed in the United States of America
under the supervision of
Rolls Offset Printing Co., Inc., N.Y.

10 9 8 7 6 5 4 3 2 1

Acknowledgments:

For this book, several greenhouses of many kinds were photographed and I sincerely want to thank the following people for allowing us to photograph their personal places for plants:

Dan Campbell
Don Worth
Ben Botelli
Carol and Red Spediacci
Dan DeGunthen
Hamilton Tyler
Western Springs Nursery

Special gratitude goes to my good friend, Eldon Danhausen, of Chicago, Illinois for photos of his greenhouse, and to the many photographers and artists who worked on this book, my thanks as always.

For reading and making suggestions on the chapters on Materials and Construction, my deepest appreciation goes to Andrew Roy Addkison, Interior Designer of the California College of Arts and Crafts of Oakland, California.

Contents

photo by Clark Photo/Graphic

Illustrations

your homemade greenhouse and how to build it

1 Gardens Under Glass- All Year Long

Years ago only the very wealthy could afford greenhouses, but now there is a greenhouse for everyone's pocketbook. Having a place for plants makes you a gardener year-round rather than just for those few months when outdoor weather is good. A greenhouse filled with colorful flowers and sprouting seeds, whether under plastic or glass, will fill your soul with warmth inside, even though it may be gray and cold outside. The greenhouse will provide a pleasant retreat from the busy world; you can sneak into your Eden any time and be in a totally new world. And of course a greenhouse will save you money because you can start plants from cuttings, grow herbs and vegetables, and start seeds to get a head start on spring.

Making Your Own Greenhouse

A greenhouse can be part of any property no matter how limited the outdoor space. *(You can even have a window greenhouse if there is no outdoor space)*. Prefabricated greenhouses, available in many sizes and styles, are fine, but building your own greenhouse has four advantages: (1) you can use whatever space is available, from 5x10 to 10x20 feet; (2) you can use imaginative designs; (3) you can make the greenery part of the house or have a detached unit; (4) and you can use old or new materials. In essence, you can save

a great deal of money by doing it yourself. Remember that a prefabricated greenhouse kit is delivered knocked down (KD), so you must put it together as well as supply the foundation *(generally a costly project)*. The greenhouse you design and build yourself (or have built) can be small or large, sophisticated or simple in design, inexpensive or costly. For example, some excellent places for plants cost only $200, and some distinctive and lovely handhewn ones cost no more than $500.

Getting Started

Just how do you go about creating and building your own greenhouse? First consider these seven questions:

(1) Where will it go?
(2) What will it be made from?
(3) What is the best design for the house?
(4) How much money can you spend?
(5) What are you going to use it for?
(6) Is it to be attached or detached?
(7) How much artificial heat will be needed?

To answer these questions, make sketches *(you do not have to be an artist)* and list the supplies and materials you will need to give you a rough cost estimate. Following are some ideas to get your imagination going. (And drawings are included throughout the book to help you.)

Attached or Detached (Second Floor?)

A greenhouse can be either attached or separate from the house, depending on what you want to use it for. If you are going to display plants, the attached unit is better because then the greenery becomes part of the house, thus increasing the space of your total living area. The attached unit may be adjacent to the living room, offering a pleasant view, off the kitchen, providing a cheerful note on dull days; off the bedroom, becoming a delightful addition to the daily living scheme; or even part of the bathroom, lending a tropical look to the bath and helping to dress up the area considerably.

The attached greenhouse offers easy accessibility to the main house in inclement weather and is an enjoyable place for morning coffee. Finally, the attached unit makes it possible to use existing heating facilities *(by adding a duct from the main furnace)* and thus cut costs. The disadvantage of the attached unit is that it is always visible to guests and thus must be kept neat to prevent it from being an eyesore.

The detached greenhouse is generally a more personal place, a place where you can actually work with rather than only display plants. It is the potting shed, the place to propagate plants, the "hospital" for those plants not in their prime. Even though it does not extend your living area, it still can be a retreat from the house if

SOLAR ANGLES

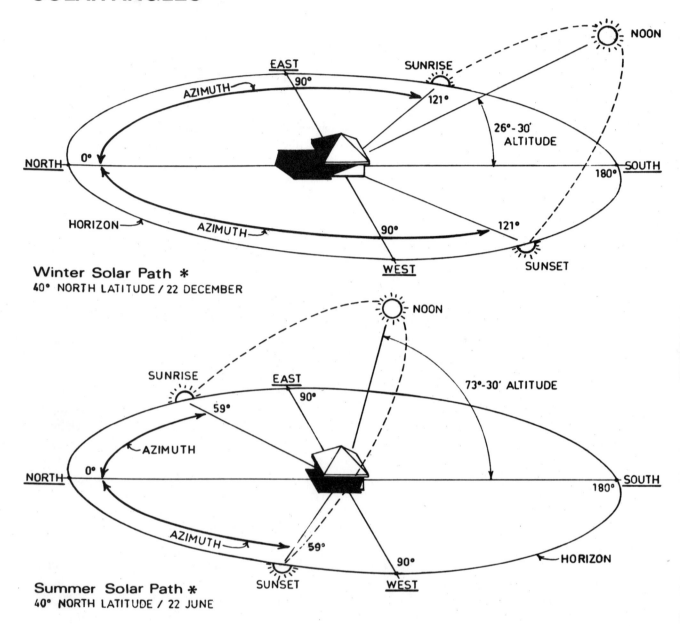

Winter Solar Path ✷
40° NORTH LATITUDE / 22 DECEMBER

Summer Solar Path ✷
40° NORTH LATITUDE / 22 JUNE

LATITUDE	SEASON	SUNRISE	SUNSET	AZIMUTH	ALTITUDE
50°	WINTER	8:00	4:00	128°-30'	16°-30'
	SUMMER	4:00	8:00	51°-30'	63°-30'
45°	WINTER	7:40	4:20	124°-30'	21°-30'
	SUMMER	4:20	7:40	55°-30'	68°-30'
✷ 40°	WINTER	7:30	4:30	121°-0'	26°-30'
	SUMMER	4:30	7:30	59°-0'	73°-30'

LATITUDE	SEASON	SUNRISE	SUNSET	AZIMUTH	ALTITUDE
35°	WINTER	7:10	4:50	119°-0'	31°-30'
	SUMMER	4:50	7:10	61°-30'	78°-30'
30°	WINTER	7:00	5:00	117°-30'	36°-30'
	SUMMER	5:00	7:00	62°-30'	83°-30'
25°	WINTER	6:50	5:10	116°-30'	41°-30'
	SUMMER	5:10	6:50	88°-30'	63°-30'

NOTE : THESE LATITUDES COVER THE CONTINENTAL UNITED STATES. HOURS INDICATED ARE STANDARD TIME. AZIMUTHS ARE AT SUNRISE AND SUNSET, NOON AZIMUTHS ARE ALWAYS 180°. NOON ALTITUDES ARE GIVEN, ALTITUDES AT SUNRISE AND SUNSET ARE ALWAYS 0°.

you want to get away from the telephone, relatives, or whatever. And the detached greenhouse unit gives you more scope in design; an A-frame or a dome, a gazebo-type or an arched structure. *(See Chapter 4 for greenhouse designs).* Because this greenhouse acts as its own entity, it does not have to match the main house *(the attached unit has to).* The detached greenhouse is a workshop of plants that can provide infinite pleasure. Two drawbacks are (1) it must have separate heating, and (2) it is difficult to get to when weather is bad.

Naturally it would be nice to have both a detached working greenhouse and a display place for plants that is part of the house, but this is rarely feasible because of cost. Why not build one one year and plan the other for the future?

Location

The enjoyment you get from your greenhouse will depend on its location to both the outdoors and the home. A greenhouse facing south will always be in sun throughout the day, regardless of latitude or season. In chilly climates this location is almost a must so you do not use too much fuel to heat the structure. In temperate climates the south location is not necessarily the best. You can modify the location by using an overhang on the greenhouse *(this will enhance, not detract from, the looks)* to eliminate direct sun during a part of the summer day and yet allow early morning and late afternoon sun into the house. In winter, when the sun is lower in the sky, the sun will strike the area from under the overhang.

I like a western exposure because it gets the right intensity of sun. Until lunch time this area is relatively bright *(good for plants)* but not blinding. In the afternoon it will receive the full force of the sun's rays, but they are less intense than those from overhead sun. Still, this greenhouse will get plenty hot about 4:00 P.M., but most plants can take this heat and like it for the few hours until the sun goes down. If the heat gets too intense, as it did in my west-facing greenhouse, add an overhang or, in severe cases, some lattice work on the west wall. In winter, without morning sun, the west-facing greenhouse is apt to be damp, especially through rainy months, so good surface drainage is essential.

The eastern greenhouse gets the excellent morning sun but cools off in the afternoon, which is the ideal situation for plants. The

When you make your own greenhouse you can build it any size or shape you want to match your home. This small L-shaped unit is in perfect proportion to the house and offers a pleasant view looking into it as well as lovely color when viewed from within the house. Sliding doors and a plastic dome furnish enough light for plants. (*Photo by Clark Photo Graphics*).

drawback is that in winter it will be quite cool and dark by afternoon and thus require more heat to sustain the plants for cold nights.

For years the northern exposure was shunned as a site for a greenhouse, but sometimes by necessity this is the only available place. What do you do? Go ahead and build it because there are ways to get more light into it. Even in summer the north greenhouse receives little or no sun, but it does get good bright light, so do not rule out the northern exposure: dozens of plants prefer bright light instead of direct sun. My new greenhouse is oriented east and north, and I find it conducive to growing many, many plants that will not take the direct sun of the south-west-oriented greenhouse at the other end of my property. Orchids in particular seem to prefer my new greenhouse; in summer many burned from direct sun in the other area.

Cost

Because materials are so expensive today, cost is a very important part of building. The average do-it-yourself greenhouse can cost as little as $200 or as much as $2,000. The one I recently added to my kitchen area—simple wood and glass construction, with a tar and gravel roof and domes for light—cost less than $700; similar units can be built easily within this budget. What you cover the basic greenhouse skeleton with determines the actual cost. For example, a covering of flexible plastic for a 10x14 greenhouse can cost no more than $60; in rigid fiberglas about $200, in glass or acrylic about $400, and so on. If you can not afford glass or acrylic at

Corrugated fiberglas in combination with wood make this structure a fine area for plants of all kinds. The wood and fiberglas greenhouse is inexpensive, easy to build, and a definite plus on any property. This greenhouse is a detached unit. (*Photo by Matthew Barr*).

Aluminum is the framework for a greenhouse. It is popular because it is easily maintained; this hipped design greenhouse is really a loft unit with a studio below. (*Photo by Pat Matsumoto*).

the start, go ahead and build the greenhouse skeleton and use a plastic or screen temporary covering; in a year or so *(when you have the money),* do the permanent installation with glass or plastic.

You can also build a greenhouse from salvaged materials; although it may not be the ultimate in appearance, it will serve to house your plants. A greenhouse of salvaged materials can be built for less than $200 if you carefully scout salvage yards.

When you build your own greenhouse, you may have many alternatives, depending on the money available at the time. The initial cost of excavating and foundation should be considered in all greenhouse building; the average concrete footing and foundation will run from $100 to $200, depending on how much labor you do yourself. The more you do, the less it will cost. Concrete footings and foundation details are explained in Chapter 3.

Heating/Water

The amount of artificial heat needed for your greenhouse depends on its size and where you live. In very cold winter regions more heating will be necessary than in, say, southern areas. Greenhouse suppliers have a large selection of heaters, none exorbitant in price and even with the increase in fuel costs, the price of heating the greenhouse will not be expensive. And for those very cold nights that may occur there are some old-fashioned ways of conserving heat within the greenhouse and we talk about these methods as well as specific applications of heaters in Chapter 6.

To determine just how much heat you will need in the green-

The loft greenhouse seen from a distance shows the interesting design. The unit faces south and provides ample light for plants. As an addition to the property it is a totally charming scene. (*Photo by Pat Matsumoto*).

This attached greenhouse is of wood and glass; it is a leanto design using the house wall as a fourth wall. Thus, the view from the kitchen is pleasing and the view from outside equally handsome. The structure faces east and north and this greenhouse owned by the author cost $700 to build. (*Photo by author*).

house you will have to know the inside temperature; this means you'll need a thermometer. Find an instrument that is both a thermometer and a hygrometer *(that measures moisture in the air)* and place it midway on a wall in the greenhouse; this way you will have both temperature and humidity readings at a glance.

Fancy equipment to provide water to your greenhouse is not necessary. In temperate climates you can, of course, use a hose connected to an outside faucet and it will cost nothing. *(In climates where winters are severe this would hardly be feasible.)* Extending the water line from an existing house line to the greenhouse is not really a costly procedure and a plumber can do it for you. If the greenhouse is detached from the house, the line must be laid beneath the ground (check freezing levels with Building Code offices), and this would involve somewhat more cost than a line from the main house to an attached greenhouse. Either way, a faucet in the greenhouse is necessary and should be considered part of the total greenhouse cost.

Prefabricated Greenhouses

Years ago if you wanted a prefabricated greenhouse you almost had to buy a metal-and-glass structure, usually a lean-to. The detached units then available were often commercial and sterile in appearance. Not so today. Now there is an array of new designs in prefabricated or knocked-down (KD) units. Many manufacturers have gone back to wood framing and there is a choice of cover materials. Domes, arches, and hexag-

onal shapes are all part of the new greenhouse scene. While the prefabricated unit is convenient—you get all the pieces—you still must put it together yourself and in the majority of cases you still must have a suitable foundation for the greenhouse which you too supply, so in essence, this is still a homemade project.

If you prefer to buy a green-

house kit and there are several suitable ones, do add a few handcrafted touches of your own to it. This can be a different kind of door or some overhead beams to give it a personal taste. Also, with any greenhouse you have, remember that glass is a poor conductor; the greenhouse will be expensive to heat in winter and very hot in summer. Consider using glass in

A homemade greenhouse of infinite charm is shown in this attached unit. Redwood is used throughout as building members and plastic fiberglas panels for a ceiling. The casement windows of the house add great beauty to the scene and the lush plantings within the greenhouse always make it an inviting place. Note the wooden door at right, in character to the total picture. *(Photo by Clark Photo Graphics).*

combination with some other material as a covering.

No matter which kind of greenhouse you select, whether it is prefabricated or homemade, and no matter where it is, you will always be able to grow plants in it. There are plants for every exposure—north, south, east, west—and we discuss them in Chapter 5.

Getting Help

There are some architects who will give you a rough sketch of your own greenhouse design for a minimal fee. However, you have to take it from there. For one of my early greenhouses I hired a local architect who did rough sketches from my pencil drawings for $50 which is hardly exorbitant. Having everything on paper made it easy for me to get started.

Some states' laws say that if you build the greenhouse yourself and the cost of material is say, under $400, no permit is needed. Other states require a permit for even an outhouse, so check and be sure. In most parts of the country law requires that you install a foundation or footing for your greenhouse. You must conform to building-codes about freezing depth and so forth and it is all for your own good. You can get help by calling your local building-code service *(listed in yellow pages)*.

Try and get help with digging and pouring the foundation. Working alone is backbreaking; get a handyman or someone to help. Few carpenters are willing to build a greenhouse, and contractors may be too busy building homes, so it might be up to you and in the following chapters we offer help and guidance to get you going with your homemade greenhouse.

An inexpensive wood and plastic-sheet greenhouse can be made in a weekend and serves many purposes. This is simple A-frame construction and affords a place for plants for less than $100. (*Photo by Matthew Barr*).

Looking into a simple wood and plastic greenhouse. (*Photo by Matthew Barr*).

2 Materials for the Greenhouse

You will be using lumber, glass, plastic, concrete, and possibly brick for your greenhouse, so it is wise to know something about them. The framing for a greenhouse is generally wood or aluminum and may be covered with flexible plastic, glass, or fiberglas panels. Plastic or glass are generally used for roofs and skylights. Floors are usually made of concrete or brick. The end of this chapter has tables for your convenience: types of plastic covering, aspects of glass use, and charts on lumber specifications.

Wood

Wood is a basic building material; it is easy to work with, can be cut and sawed, nailed and drilled by even the average person. It is available in a mind-boggling array of sizes, species, and grades. You should be acquainted with some of the basic wood information because wood will be the framing for your greenhouse unless you use prefab metal units or salvaged materials. Recently there has been a return to wood because it is more charming and better looking than metal, which can be quite sterile in appearance. With wood, you can use curved lines if necessary and have more latitude in design, especially in regards to greenhouse construction.

Woods are generally divided into two types: hardwood, such as oak, maple, beech; and soft-

woods, such as cedar, redwood, and pine. Hardwood, more durable and harder to work with than softwood, is usually used for floors or furniture construction. Softwoods are easy to work with and so for our purposes are the best materials.

Redwood and cedar heartwood lumber is more resistant to decay than most other woods. It can take an awful lot of moisture and yet last for years; has an inherent acid preservative, and is more termite proof than most woods. Douglas fir is good too, and cypress *(if you can find it)* has exceptional qualities. Generally, even with redwood, wood preservatives or paint will be needed to further ensure long-lasting qualities. There are various grades of lumber to consider; see the charts at the end of this section.

Wood Preservatives

Preservatives will lengthen the life of any wood because they will protect the woods from moisture. There are many wood preservatives available at hardware and paint stores. The best ones are the

pentachlorophenol forms, which are sold under a variety of trade names. They make wood almost perfectly resistant to water penetration; for example, Penta is water repellent and can be painted. Wood preservatives can injure skin, so handle them carefully: wear gloves, try not to get any on your hands, and follow to the letter the directions on the can.

A good quality paint will further protect wood. Because there are so many paints available, it is impossible to discuss them here. Tell your paint dealer that the paint will be used for greenhouse construction and let him guide you accordingly.

Buying Lumber

If at all possible, design the greenhouse so the length of lumber parts—rafters, beams, and posts—are in even numbers because lumber is sold on the even inch. Always use, if you can, even-numbered lumber. Odd sizes are not always in stock and have to be cut from even sizes, in which case you must pay for the longer size and the cutting of the wood.

Standard Dimensions of Surfaced Lumber

Size to Order	Surfaced Actual Size	
	Unseasoned	Dry
2 X 3	1 9/16 X 2 9/16	1 1/2 X 2 1/2
2 X 4	1 9/16 X 3 9/16	1 1/2 X 3 1/2
2 X 6	1 9/16 X 5 5/8	1 1/2 X 5 1/2
2 X 8	1 9/16 X 7 1/2	1 1/2 X 7 1/4
2 X 10	1 9/16 X 9 1/2	1 1/2 X 9 1/4
2 X 12	1 9/16 X 11 1/2	1 1/2 X 11 1/4

BASIC GLASS INSTALLATION - WOOD

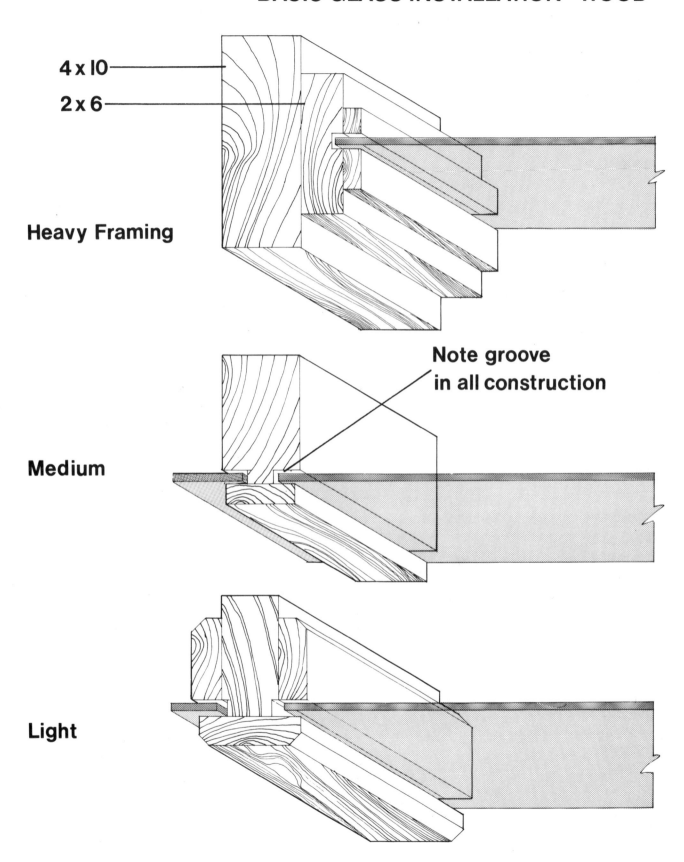

4 x 10

2 x 6

Heavy Framing

Note groove
in all construction

Medium

Light

BASIC GLASS INSTALLATION - METAL

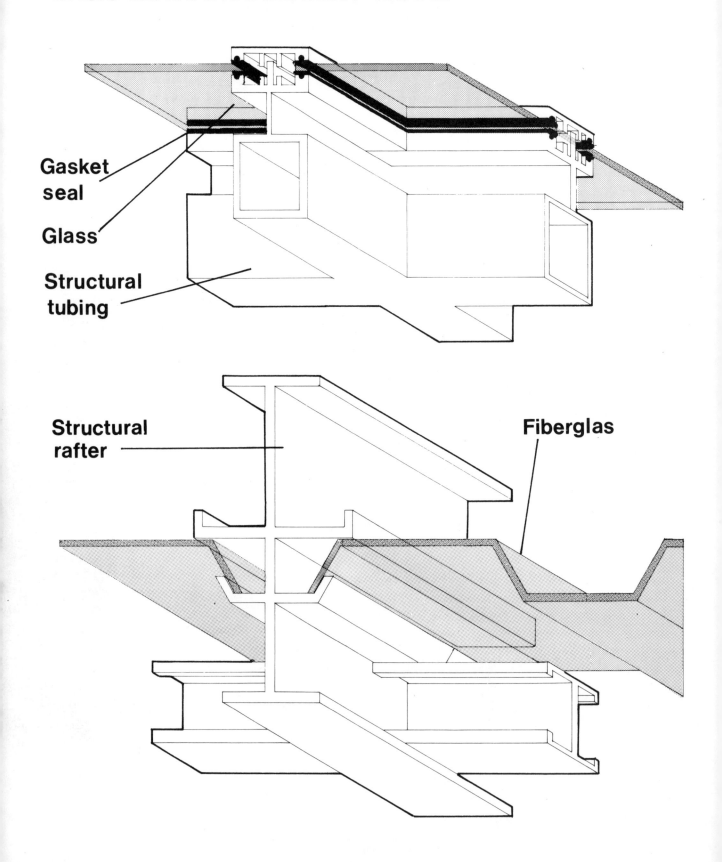

Gasket
seal

Glass

Structural
tubing

Structural
rafter

Fiberglas

When you design the roof, know at the start what roofing material you will be using; glass, acrylic, or fiberglas. Spacing and structural support depend on the weight. When buying lumber, specify exactly what grade you want and the size and length needed. State quantity first, type of wood, size, and then length.

Glass

For years the standard greenhouse glass sizes were 16 X 20 and 18 X 24. Today, these sizes are still used, but they are no longer mandatory.

Greenhouse glass is designated SSB *(single strength B grade)* or DSB *(double strength B grade)*. SSB is 1/16 inch thick; DSB is 1/8 inch thick. The B designation does not mean that much as opposed to the A or top-quality type. DSB and SSB *(commonly called window glass)* is available on the even inch in boxes of 50 or 100 square feet, so a box of glass 16 X 20 would contain fourteen pieces *(lites)*. Greenhouse glass may also be 3/16 or even 7/32 inch thick; naturally these thicknesses weigh and cost more.

Glass *must* be glazed properly. The glass must fit precisely the aluminum or wooden opening. Glazing compound is put around the edges to seal the glass, and generally a moulding *(or a capping if aluminum is used)* is set in place. If properly installed, glass is leakproof, which is of utmost importance in greenhouse construction.

In some states, if you use glass to ground units, you will have to use tempered or wire glass at ground level or moullion bars at

Kinds of Lumber

Grades	Redwood Clear	Red Cedar	Douglas Fir
Top grade; expensive; used mostly for cabinetry Structural members for heavy construction	All heart	C and better finishes	C and better finishes
Excellent for most uses; only slight defects	Select heart	C finishes	C finishes
Suitable for general construction; has some knots and defects; economical, but should be painted	Construction heart	Merchantable construction	Construction

Note: Lumber comes in grades such as A, B, C, D; A denotes top quality.

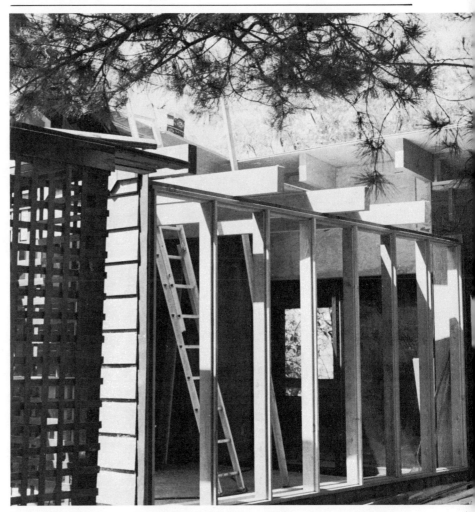

Redwood has been used extensively for this small greenhouse. Note that the window members shown are rabbetted (notched) to provide space for glass. This type of construction also eliminates leakage possibilities. To assure moisture from entering wood, all wooden members were given a protective clear coating and then two coats of paint. (*Photo by author*).

least 16 inches above ground level for safety reasons. Tempered glass is five times as strong as standard glass and comes in various thicknesses: 3/16, 7/32, and 1/4 inch. Tempered glass breaks into small pieces, thus avoiding serious accidents. Wire glass is clear glass with wire inserts. If it breaks, the glass adheres to the wire rather than cracking into large pieces.

Glazing Compounds

There is a host of new glazing compounds on the market. But investigate before you buy because the right glazing material can mean the difference between a lot of maintenance or little maintenance. The newer compounds are hard on the outside but remain pliable inside, which is a definite plus. They also have a longer life and are extremely easy to install with a glazing gun.

The mastic-type compounds are good, but the plastic types are even better. Putty, which for so many years has been used to install glass, should be avoided because it becomes brittle and then falls away in a year or so. And using a putty knife to glaze with, is much more difficut than using a glazing gun.

Plastic

Flexible

Polyethylene, the most used flexible plastic, comes in cones of 2, 4, and 6 mil thicknesses, in a variety of widths. The heavier the plastic, the longer its life. Do not expect any polyethylene skin to last more than 1 year.

Glass is used in combination with plastic windows in this greenhouse. The small panes of glass are easy to install and the egg-crate framing adds charm to the unit. (*Photo by Matthew Barr*).

PLASTIC SCREEN GREENHOUSE

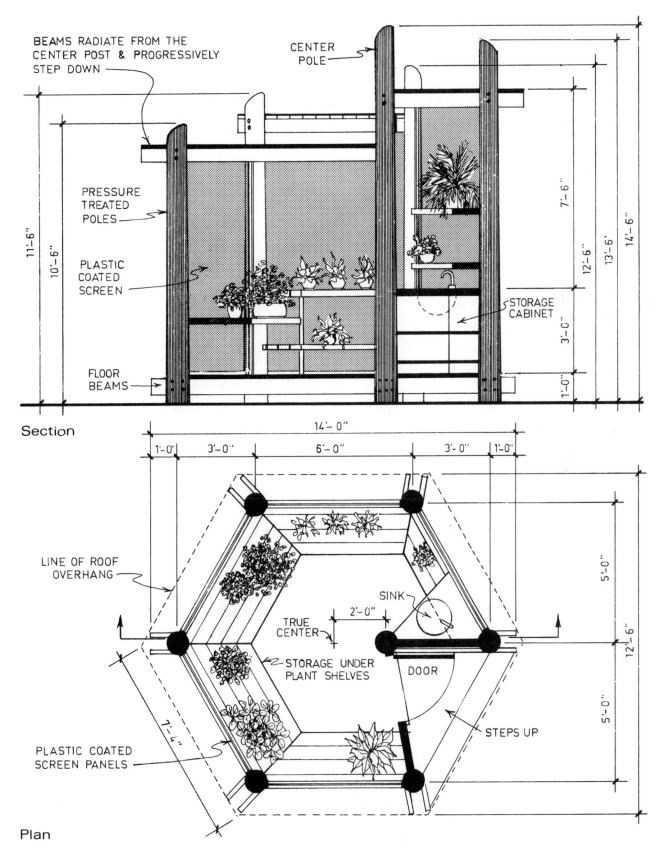

BEAMS RADIATE FROM THE
CENTER POST & PROGRESSIVELY
STEP DOWN

CENTER
POLE

PRESSURE
TREATED
POLES

PLASTIC
COATED
SCREEN

STORAGE
CABINET

FLOOR
BEAMS

11'-6"

10'-6"

7'-6"

13'-6"

14'-6"

12'-6"

3'-0"

1'-0"

Section

14'-0"

1'-0"   3'-0"   6'-0"   3'-0"   1'-0"

LINE OF ROOF
OVERHANG

TRUE
CENTER

SINK

2'-0"

STORAGE UNDER
PLANT SHELVES

DOOR

STEPS UP

PLASTIC COATED
SCREEN PANELS

7'-4"

5'-0"

12'-6"

5'-0"

Plan

GREENHOUSE WITH ACRYLIC

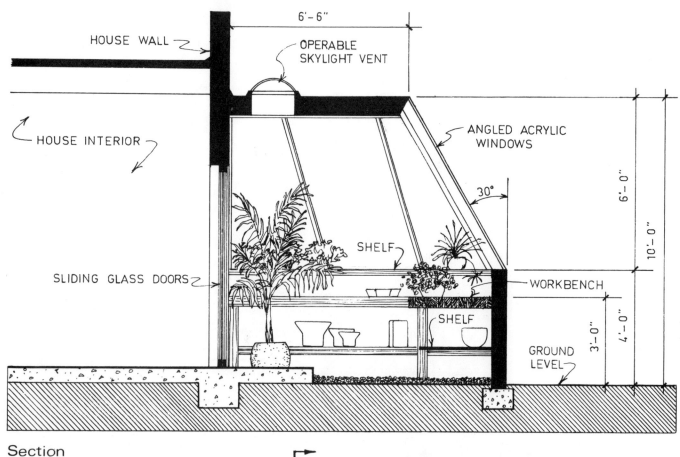

HOUSE WALL

6'- 6"

OPERABLE
SKYLIGHT VENT

HOUSE INTERIOR

ANGLED ACRYLIC
WINDOWS

30°

6'- 0"

10'- 0"

SHELF

SLIDING GLASS DOORS

WORKBENCH

SHELF

4'- 0"

3'- 0"

GROUND
LEVEL

Section

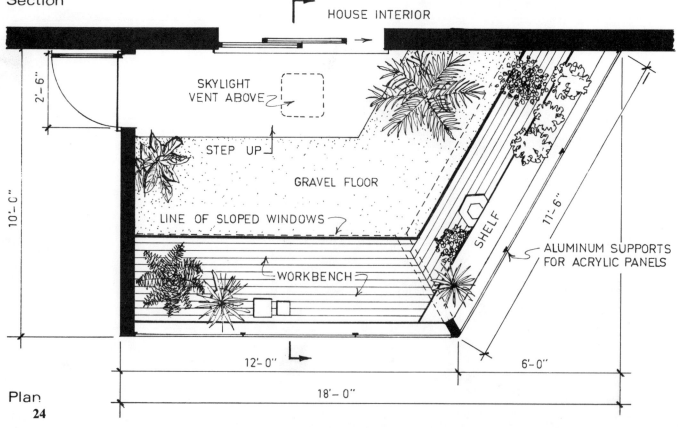

HOUSE INTERIOR

2'- 6"

SKYLIGHT
VENT ABOVE

STEP UP

GRAVEL FLOOR

10'- 0"

LINE OF SLOPED WINDOWS

11'- 6"

SHELF

ALUMINUM SUPPORTS
FOR ACRYLIC PANELS

WORKBENCH

12'- 0"

6'- 0"

18'- 0"

Plan

Vinyl plastic comes in 8 mil thicknesses, in 36, 48, and 60 inch widths. It is more costly than polyethylene but lasts about twice as long. However, in extreme cold it becomes brittle.

Polyester plastic is available in 3 or 5 mil thicknesses. This is about the best flexible plastic, sometimes lasting as long as 3 years. It requires overlapping and should be stretched as tightly as possible on the frame to eliminate noise rattle.

Fiberglas

The fiberglas sheet panel, corrugated or flat, is a simple answer to installation and cost for greenhouse roofing or siding. Also, it is easy to work with because it is lightweight, and it can be drilled and sawed, even by the novice. Its one disadvantage is that is it not always esthetically pleasing, but if properly framed and detailed, it can be quite handsome.

Panels are either brightly colored or translucent; either type admits sufficient subdued light for most plants, which is excellent for plant growth. I prefer the translucent panels because they are more natural looking, and the corrugated panel is easier to install than the flat one.

Because the corrugated panel is the most popular, we shall outline its installation; except for the overlapping principle, most other fiberglas panels can be installed in the same manner.

The 26-inch panel is the most

Plastic flexible coverings can be used for greenhouse skeletons but at best are only temporary and will have to be replaced with other materials. Still, if money is short this is the way to go because flexible plastic is inexpensive and does offer some protection from the elements. (*Photo by author*).

25

CORRUGATED FIBERGLAS GREENHOUSE

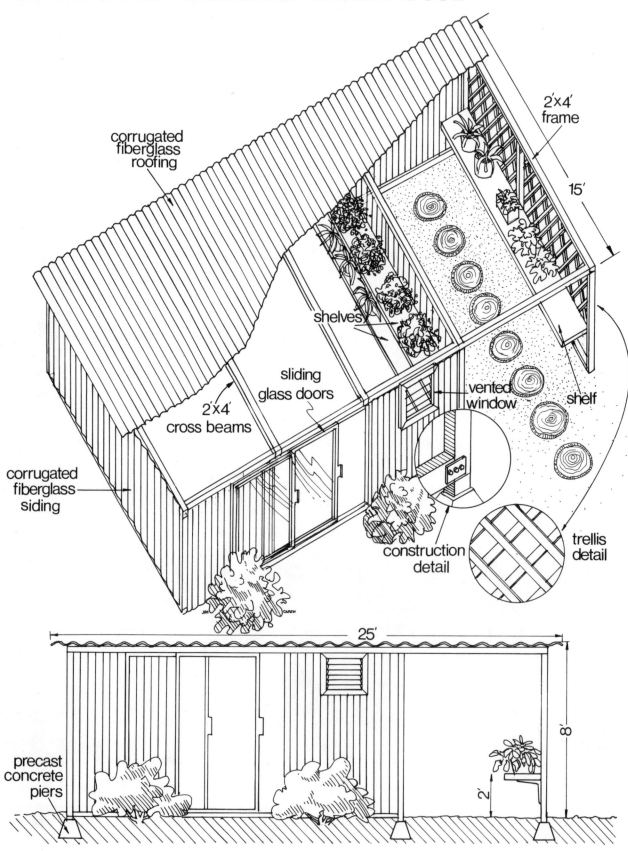

corrugated
fiberglass
roofing

2'x4'
frame

15'

shelves

sliding
glass doors

vented
window

shelf

2'x4'
cross beams

corrugated
fiberglass
siding

construction
detail

trellis
detail

JIM   CAREW

25'

8'

precast
concrete
piers

2'

This small L-shaped greenhouse is glazed with flat fiberglas panels of natural color; combined with the white painted wood framing it is esthetically pleasing and functional. (*Photo by Clark Photo Graphics*).

common size; this provides a 2-inch overlap on rafters spaced 2 feet on centers. Use wood members to support the panels along the seams. You should also use cross bracing, every 5 feet between the rafters, to support the panels so they do not sag. Thus an eggcrate-type framing system ideally suits panels.

As previously mentioned, try to build your greenhouse roof or sides with standard-sized materials to avoid time-consuming cutting. If you have to cut, use a fine-toothed hand saw. Fiberglas panels can be nailed, but do use the nails made especially for fiberglas; they have a rubber washer that eliminates the possibility of crazing around the nail hole. Nail panels every 12 inches, driving the nails through the crowns rather than the valleys of the corrugation. You can also use special wood screws *(sold at dealers)* instead of nails. Be sure and first apply mastic sealant between the panels whether using nails or screws.

Occasionally hose down panels with clear water to eliminate dirt and soot buildup. You can resurface the panels by rubbing them with pads of soft steel wool, working lengthwise along the corrugations. When panels are thoroughly dry, apply a liquid resin that dries to a smooth, tough finish which provides a strong outer skin over the original surface.

Corrugated fiberglas panels are used for this detached greenhouse. Overlapped and on redwood frames they make an excellent covering; these are light green in color. (*Photo by Matthew Barr*).

Glass Data

Material	Thickness, type	Installation	Standard Size	Remarks
Window glass DSB	1/8 inch thick rolled glass	Glazing compound and clips	16 X 18, in 2 inch increments	Best for average size greenhouse; maximum size 30 X 40.
Window glass SSB	1/16 inch thick rolled glass	Glazing compound and clips	16 X 18, in 2 inch increments	Cheaper than above but not as good; maximum size 24 X 30.
Wire glass	1/4 inch thick; wire embedded	Glazing compound and clips	4 to 12 feet long, in 2 inch increments	Necessary for skylights; looks good. Can be used in any size.
Tempered glass	1/4 inch thick; clear	Glazing compound and clips	Many sizes (*check with dealer*)	Necessary for skylights. Sometimes warps; stay with small sizes.

Plastic Covering for Skelton Framing

Material	Description	Installation	Standard Sizes	Remarks
Flexible Plastic	Almost clear	Stapling gun	24 to 48 inch width rolls	Temporary
Fiberglas panels	Strong rigid sheets; flat or corrugated; in colors or almost clear	Nailed or screwed in	20 to 36 inch wide, 60, 72 or 96 inches long	Can last several years
Saran shade cloth	Plastic, with many densities	Tacks or stapling gun	24 to 60 inch widths	Temporary
Plastic screen	Wire embedded in plastic	Staple gun	35 inch width rolls	Can last a year or more; looks okay
Aluminum and plastic	Gray, plastic-coated aluminum wires	Nailed to wood frame	24 to 48 inch width rolls	Looks okay; can last about a year

3 Construction of the Greenhouse

Whether you design and build your own room or have a designer or contractor do it for you, some basic information about construction will provide you with a background so you can construct a functional room. The following information will enable you to talk knowingly to carpenters or contractors and/or show you how to build your own room.

Footings

First you must consider footings and foundations because they anchor the greenhouse to the ground *(a footing is part of the foundation)*. Footings can be of slab construction, a footings-and-foundation wall, used with a masonry wall, concrete tubes, or precast piers. Several types of footings are shown in Drawings. Designs may vary depending upon where you live and building codes, but the following general plan can be used:

1. Drive twelve stakes or four batten boards 4 to 8 feet from the proposed corners. Lay out the exact plan of the building with string from stake to stake or board to board.

2. Dig a trench approximately 2 feet wide and a minimum of 1 foot deep *(or whatever building codes advise)* around the perimeter of the proposed site.

3. Decide what height the foundation footing will be, and then use a level to make sure all batten boards or stakes are on the same level.

4. Rent foundation framing equipment, or use 3/4-inch plywood. The width of the footing should be 8 inches or whatever local building codes require.

5. If the room is to be a heavy structure, reinforce footings with steel rods inlaid horizontally and vertically. Pound the vertical rods into the ground between the foundation framing and then tie the horizontal rods *(use wires)* to the vertical ones.

6. Leave 1/4- to 1/2-inch D anchor bolts (available at lumber yards) protruding from the top of the footing as a base for nailing in upright members. The length of the bolt depends upon the size of the bearing plate you use, but be sure to allow for a longer rather than a short bolt. Lay the bearing plate approximately 1 inch inside the outside line of the footing.

7. Apply mastic to the top of the footing to stop capillary action.

8. Be sure there is adequate drainage. Leave 3-inch holes in the foundation base about every 6 feet so water can run off to a lower grade.

9. For outside drainage, place drain tiles at the base and through the footings, on 4 to 6 inches of rough gravel.

10. For inside drainage, plan a floor drain *(optional)*. Before floor is installed. Locate the drainage heads in a low area. The drain-pipe should extend all around the exterior of the room at the base of the footing in trench.

As mentioned, the above information is for general footing and foundation work. You can in some instances use precase concrete piers *(sold at suppliers)* as footings for say, lightweight greenhouses, and then the flooring material would be cinders, gravel, or earth.

The Frame

The frame or skeleton of your greenhouse is your next construction consideration. You can use the traditional aluminum, but it is sterile looking. Some manufacturers of prefabricated greenhouses have started offering anodized colored aluminum, which is somewhat better. The structural elements of these prefabs are made of aluminum alloy or hot-dip galvanized steel. You do not have to paint aluminum, and the metal does not deteriorate. However, besides its sterile look, aluminum has another drawback: heat loss is greater than with wood, so heating an aluminum greenhouse can be expensive.

Thus, there has been a return to the use of wood. An objection to wood for a greenhouse has been that it rots because of the water and humidity. But today's excellent wood preservatives and paints overcome most problems. Definitely consider building your green-

CONCRETE DETAILS

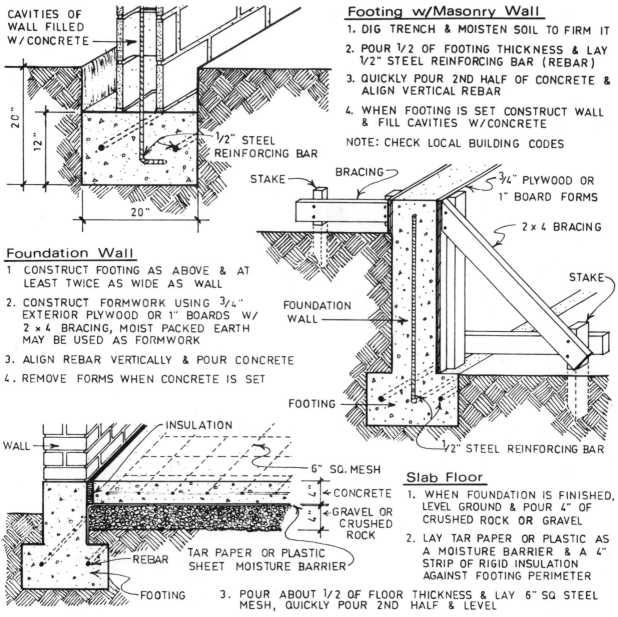

CAVITIES OF WALL FILLED W/CONCRETE

1/2" STEEL REINFORCING BAR

20"

12"

20"

Footing w/Masonry Wall

1. DIG TRENCH & MOISTEN SOIL TO FIRM IT

2. POUR 1/2 OF FOOTING THICKNESS & LAY 1/2" STEEL REINFORCING BAR (REBAR)

3. QUICKLY POUR 2ND HALF OF CONCRETE & ALIGN VERTICAL REBAR

4. WHEN FOOTING IS SET CONSTRUCT WALL & FILL CAVITIES W/CONCRETE

NOTE: CHECK LOCAL BUILDING CODES

STAKE

BRACING

3/4" PLYWOOD OR 1" BOARD FORMS

2 x 4 BRACING

STAKE

FOUNDATION WALL

FOOTING

1/2" STEEL REINFORCING BAR

Foundation Wall

1. CONSTRUCT FOOTING AS ABOVE & AT LEAST TWICE AS WIDE AS WALL

2. CONSTRUCT FORMWORK USING 3/4" EXTERIOR PLYWOOD OR 1" BOARDS W/ 2 x 4 BRACING, MOIST PACKED EARTH MAY BE USED AS FORMWORK

3. ALIGN REBAR VERTICALLY & POUR CONCRETE

4. REMOVE FORMS WHEN CONCRETE IS SET

WALL

INSULATION

6" SQ. MESH

CONCRETE

GRAVEL OR CRUSHED ROCK

TAR PAPER OR PLASTIC SHEET MOISTURE BARRIER

REBAR

FOOTING

Slab Floor

1. WHEN FOUNDATION IS FINISHED, LEVEL GROUND & POUR 4" OF CRUSHED ROCK OR GRAVEL

2. LAY TAR PAPER OR PLASTIC AS A MOISTURE BARRIER & A 4" STRIP OF RIGID INSULATION AGAINST FOOTING PERIMETER

3. POUR ABOUT 1/2 OF FLOOR THICKNESS & LAY 6" SQ STEEL MESH, QUICKLY POUR 2ND HALF & LEVEL

Footing Slab

1. DIG TRENCH & LEVEL FLOOR AREA

2. SET FORMWORK AROUND PERIMETER

3. POUR 4" OF GRAVEL OR CRUSHED ROCK COVER W/ TAR PAPER OR PLASTIC SHEET

4. POUR CONCRETE & LAY REINFORCING BARS & STEEL MESH AT APPROPIATE LEVELS

5. LEVEL FLOOR & REMOVE FORMS WHEN CONCRETE IS SET

2 x 6 FORM

STAKE & BRACING

6" SQ. MESH

12"

12"

10"

TAR PAPER OR PLASTIC OVER GRAVEL

house of redwood, cedar, cypress, or Douglas fir.

The framing for your greenhouse is actually the walls, and knowing the difference between a bearing and nonbearing wall is vital before you start any building project. Bearing parts carry the weight of the structure; nonbearing walls do not. Thus, all exterior walls that run perpendicular to ceiling and floor joints are bearing.

The frame of your greenhouse should be made from seasoned lumber *(for durability)* that holds nails readily and does not warp or twist. Douglas fir is often used, although redwood is the best. There are two kinds of framing involved in greenhouse construction: western and balloon. Western framing is easy to build, works well because it resists shrinkage, and is preferred for simple greenhouses. Balloon framing is used where masonry covers walls because settlement at joints will not be as severe as with western framing. Mud sills, sole plates, headers for window framing, and wall studs are the basic components of framing. Roof framing includes rafters, beams, and posts.

Posts

Generally, use 4 X 4 inch redwood posts *(vertical supports)* for very large structures; use larger posts *(6 X 6 inch)* to support heavy roof loads and still maintain post spacing. Heavy roof loads must be considered in any area with heavy snows.

To determine how much weight your posts will hold, calculate the area of the roof supported by each post. Take the area bounded by lines drawn halfway between the post and any adjoining post or wall. Then multiply the area by roof-loading figures for your specific area *(get these from local building offices)*. For example, in most climates *(but not all)* a 40-pound per square foot load will provide a safe load figure.

Beams

To determine the size beam *(horizontal support)* needed for greenhouse construction, use the following rule of thumb: for a 4 X 4-foot span, a 4 X 4-inch beam is fine; for a 6-foot span use a 4- X 6-inch beam; for an 8-foot span use a 4- X 8-inch beam, and so on. You must use heavy beams for greenhouses with glass because glass is heavy. Lighter beams are fine for plastic covered greenhouses or small ones. Because each climate varies as to the amount of snow load, as previously mentioned check local building departments to determine the necessary dimensions for beams.

Footings and foundations are needed for most greenhouses, or at least concrete piers for lightweight ones. Note reinforcing rods used. Concrete will be poured flush with wood framing. This foundation was for a greenhouse 20 x 26 feet. Smaller units would not need such extensive walls. *(Photo by Dilday).*

BASIC CONSTUCTION - FOOTINGS AND RAFTERS

A   Footings

1   CONCRETE COLLAR
2   POST ANCHOR
3   NAILING BLOCK
4   DRIFT PIN

B   Rafters

1   TOENAIL
2   NOTCH RAFTERS
3   LEDGER
4   TOENAIL
5   JOIST HANGER

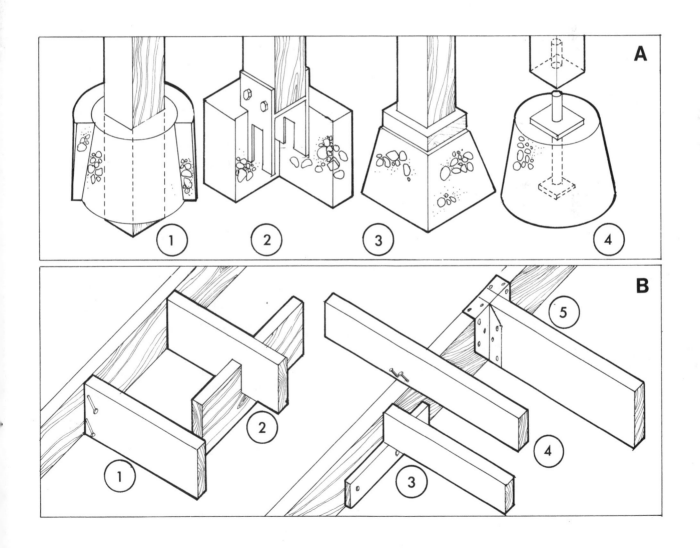

Rafters

To determine the size of the rafters needed, take the length of the rafter and the center-to-center spacing. A 2- X 4-inch rafter on a 16-inch center is fine, or use a 2 X 6 X 8 feet on 24-inch centers. Always try to use select heart California redwood or Douglas fir. These woods are strong and smooth and free of ragged surfaces where fungus and rot could collect from excessive moisture which is prevalent in all greenhouses.

Roofing

The roof, one of the most important parts of a greenhouse, may be gabled, A -framed, vaulted, sawtoothed, or more commonly, a lean-to, placed at an angle against a house wall. If the roof is all glass, it can admit too much direct sun and burn plants, so use only about 30 percent glass in the roof. This admits plenty of light for plants. The rest of the roof can be tar-and-gravel or shingles or any other roofing material.

The glass area may be glass panes set in wood panels, commercial or custom-made skylights, or plastic domes. Proper installation of glass in wood panels is difficult because leakage always seems a problem. Even custom made, these units are apt to leak so be forwarned. Also remember that building codes require tempered or wire glass in roof construction.

If you use glass in wood panels you will have to make your own or have them custom made by a mill house. Commercial skylights are at building suppliers (see yellow pages of your phone book),

and plastic domes (which are generally leakproof) are at glass stores. Ask for brochures on these materials to determine sizes available.

A good roof for greenhouse construction is one made of 2 X 4 redwood rafters, rabetted (notched out) to accommodate glass panes. Use 16 X 20, 18 X 20, or 20 X 24-inch glass; anything larger will be difficult to handle. Prime the wood members with a preservative. When this is dry, put caulking compound into a squeegee-type plunger; pump the caulking compound along the V shoulder of the wooden member. Now lay glass into the caulking bed, carefully using your palms. Leave a 1/16-inch space on each side between glass and wood so the caulking will squeeze up at the juncture of wood and glass as the pane is being set in place. Scrape away excess material. Put in lathing over this; nail in the lathing.

Overlapping panes of glass are frequently used in greenhouse construction, but this is bothersome, ugly looking, but causes less leakage. Make individual framing if you want for each piece of glass; this way you can dictate the size of the glass and use any size you want rather than being restricted to specific sizes, although some leakage might occur.

Always pitch roofs slightly so excess water drains freely.

Skylights, (glass and plastic)

Glass skylights come in a range of shapes: single pitched, double pitched, hipped, gabled, hipped with ridge ventilators, and flat. The glass is usually glazed in

metal, but wooden members can be used instead. Commercial skylights are available, but generally you will have to have skylights made to size by sheet-metal houses to accommodate specific needs. As a rule, custom-made skylights are expensive, so if at all possible use commercial industrial factory skylights, which are cheaper. You can do your own glazing; just remember to use tempered or wire glass, as explained previously, to prevent accidents. (Exceptions are prefabricated greenhouses, which come with standard glass.) Many skylights leak, so glaze very carefully. Install glass on a caulking bed in the precast frame. Read instructions on caulking compound packages carefully and heed them. If your glass is 1/4 inch thick, a suitable 1/4-inch groove must be part of the skylight members.

Installing a glass skylight frame is not easy because you must be precise. Leave an opening in the roof to accommodate the outside dimensions of the frame. Put in wooden headers and blocking, usually 2 X 4s but heavier if the skylight is large. Fit the skylight over this wooden frame, making sure it is flush so no air enters. It is important that your framing (blocks and header) are as absolutely square as the skylight. Apply mastic or caulking at the roof line, put the skylight in place with screws.

The preformed or molded plastic skylight is a handsome addition and provides maximum light for plants. Acrylic plastic is available in several shapes and sizes; it is impervious to weather, lightweight, and easy to build with. Acrylic plastic skylights are

ROOF VARIATIONS

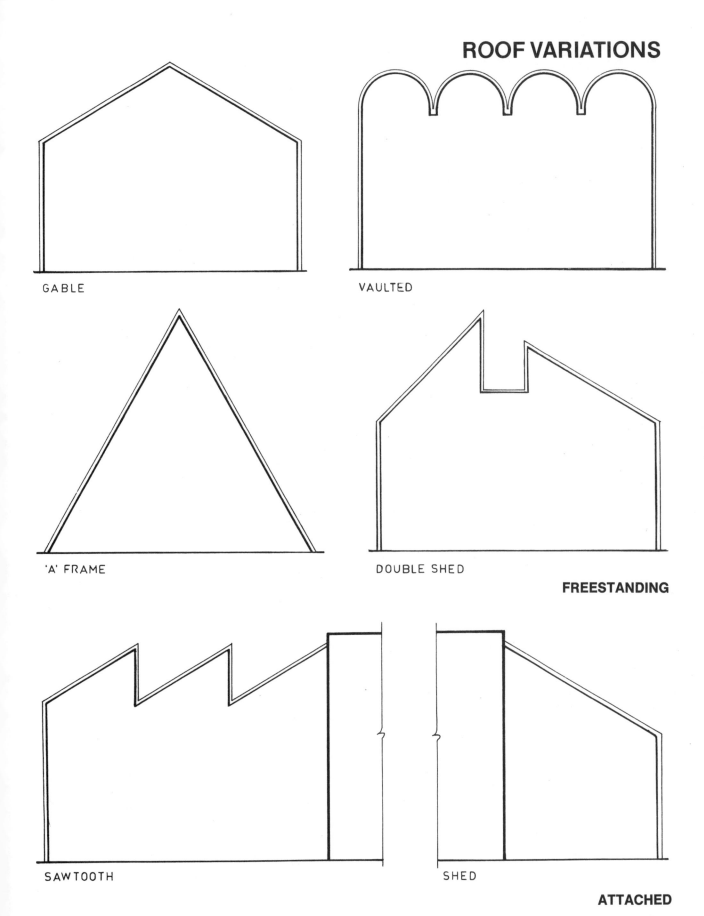

GABLE

VAULTED

'A' FRAME

DOUBLE SHED

FREESTANDING

SAWTOOTH

SHED

ATTACHED

35

SKYLIGHT DESIGNS - PLASTIC

Dome

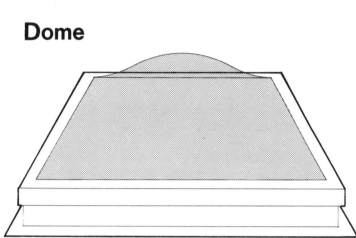

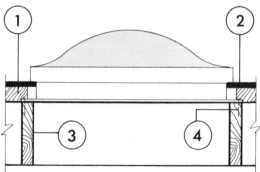

1   PLANKING
2   ROOFING PAPER
3   JOIST
4   NAIL OR SCREW

Pyramid

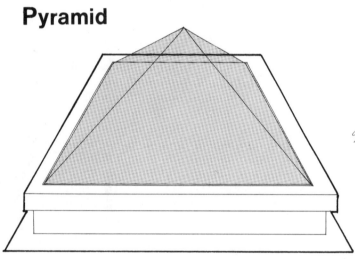

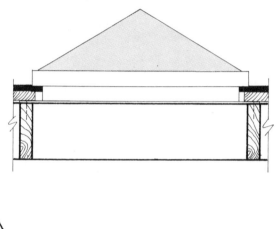

Slope

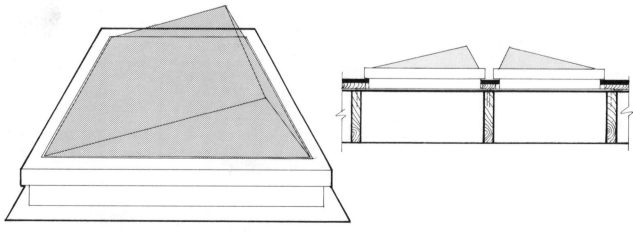

domed, right angled, peaked, or triangular. The dome shape comes in 37 X 37 standard, 48 X 48, and so forth. The other designs may not be in stock but can be ordered by your glass or plastic dealer.

For an average greenhouse, say, 10 X 15 feet, you can get plenty of light with only two 37-inch domes. The larger the greenhouse the more domes you will need; the design of your greenery will dictate what shape to use.

Lathing

Lathing deserves a special section because it is such a versatile and inexpensive material to use for greenhouse construction. Laths are wooden strips used primarily as a surface for plastering. They are sold in bundles; redwood lathing is generally available in most areas. When covered with *flexible plastic,* lathing supplies a convenient temporary greenhouse at low cost. Because laths can be spaced to your dimensions and easily sawed, you can construct many different designs, from a square to a sophisticated dome.

Lathing is lightweight, so extensive foundation work is not required. Simple footings available at lumber yards can be used, with 4 X 4 posts as main supports spaced 24 inches on center *(depending on the size of the greenhouse).* The most satisfactory lathing is either redwood or red cedar heartwood because these woods are naturally weather resistant, do not need painting, and their straight grains make them less liable to warp or split. Common lath thicknesses are about 3/8 X 1-5/8 inches, sold in

lengths of 4, 6, and 8 feet in bundles of fifty pieces. Battens, which can also be used for lightweight greenhouse construction, are somewhat larger than laths: 1/4 to 3/4 inch in thickness, with widths of 2 to 3 inches, usually available in 6 or 8 foot lengths in bundles of thirty pieces. Lathing or battens can be put in place over regular post and beam construction.

Connecting to the House

For lean-to greenhouses the house wall is the fourth wall, or use the eave or the roof as a connecting point. Remember to place the roof line high enough so it clears swinging door and windows. If the eaves are low to the ground and you are using 6- or 8-inch rafters, you may have to attach your overhead above the eave line to gain needed clearance.

Attaching to the house wall itself is the general procedure and the easiest method. Carefully remove exterior finish of wall; securely fasten a long board (ledger) to the wall studs.

Rest the rafter ends on top of the ledger and then toenail them in place; a ledger can be 2 X 6 or

Rafter and ceiling supports are shown in this photo. Treated Douglas fir was used. The egg-crate design of the ceiling makes application of fiberglas easy. (*Photo by Matthew Barr*).

Basic greenhouse construction is well displayed here: beams, rafters, and a slightly pitched ceiling so there is proper water runoff. The foundation in this case is concrete blocks. (*Photo by Matthew Barr*).

This is simple A frame construction; the skeleton is then set on a foundation of concrete block (at left) and the greenhouse can be glazed with plastic or glass. This is simple inexpensive building. (*Photo by author*).

heavier if necessary. The rafters have to support both their own weight over open space without sagging and the weight of the roof, so they must be strong and sturdy. For example, a 2 X 4 is not heavy enough to hold the weight. A 2 X 6 or, better, a 2 X 8 is more satisfactory. The rafters will also require bracing at each end and in the center to keep them in line so they do not twist or sag; use two 2 X 6 or 2 X 8 blocks.

Remember to slope the roof so water can roll off. For roof slope figure 1/4 inch per every foot. Cut a triangular piece off the rafter end where it rests on the ledger strip and on the beam. Cut out the notches and fit the rafter in place to see if it is right. Use the first rafter as a template to make the others. Toenail the rafter in place, and use a sealer preservative at the joint before nailing the rafter in place. Put in metal flashing *(sheet metal or weather stripping)* at the joint. Now replace house wall boards over flashing to meet roof of greenhouse.

If you are using skylights in the roof, follow this procedure. Most skylights on lean-to greenhouses cover three roof joists *(beams)*; remove these joists and reframe with a header *(beam)* and blocking *(a support)*. Make an opening about 1/4 inch larger than the metal part of the skylight; this opening should accommodate your wall board. Now install vertical 2 X 4s between the ceiling and rafters; cut the 2 X 4s at an angle so they fit against the rafters. Nail together the 2 X 4s and rafters and toenail to joints. Pull back and cut away the roofing material—shingles or otherwise. Put wallboard in place on each side from finished roof to ceiling level. Install the plastic fixture on the roof and nail it in place, or fasten according to manufacturer's directions. Caulk and seal it. For flat roofs, use only headers and blocking. Set the skylight unit over headers and blocking, nail in place, and seal with caulking.

Doors and Sliding Units

Doors for greenhouses need not be elaborate or special; standard sized wooden doors *(at dealers)* can be used satisfactorily. Or if you want more charm in the greenhouse, use a casement-type door. The framing and hanging of the door *(once left to professionals)* is no longer a problem because factory-built, prehung door frames are at dealers. And framing for the door is simple to install.

The first thing to remember when framing your door is that the framing must be square. Slip the pre-hung door, which is like a box, into a stud-framed opening *(depending on door size)* and then secure it. You will also need a sill and threshold for the door; the sill slopes away from the door at the base to keep out water, and the threshold covers the opening between the bottom edge of the door and the floor.

Above the door, put in place a header, usually two 2 X 4s on edge, or use a 4 X 4. Place trimmer studs against the full-length framing studs on each side of the door. To hang the door, be sure the stud opening is slightly larger than the size of the prehung frame to allow space to shim the frame so it is exactly plumb and level. *(Shims are shingles or wedges of wood driven between the frame*

and trimmer and also below the header.) After framing is nailed in place, break off the shim flush with the trimmer studs. Nail casing trim against the opening to both the trimmer studs and the frames edges. Miter the mouldings at the top corners.

Sliding metal or wooden doors are popular and come in a wide range of sizes and quality. Sliding doors have either bottom or top rollers. To order your doors, tell the dealer the size of the opening. Like a standard door, sliders need trimmer studs on each side and a header on top, generally a 4 X 4, or heavier if the span is long.

Fiberglas ceilings eliminate any need for domes or skylights and yet affords plenty of light for plants. It is an inexpensive and good way to build the ceiling. Always pitch the roof slightly to allow for water runoff.
(Photo by Clark Photo Graphics).

Set the door frame in position so it is against the trimmer stud. Put screws in loosely through the frame into the studs and also into the header beam so the door is in place while you make necessary adjustments. There should be about 1/2 inch space between the door frame and the header, a 1/4-inch between sides and studs. Now determine which side of the opening is the locking side; shim between the frame and trimmer stud on that side. Once the blocking and shimming is done, tighten and secure the frame in place.

Flooring

Concrete

Concrete is an economical and durable floor material because it resists stains and water and will retain heat. To build your concrete floor you will need wooden forms, that is, forms to hold the concrete until it sets. You can build your own forms, but it is easier to rent them, or use steel stake forms. Put the forms in place absolutely level, with the top wood board floor level. Reinforcing steel rods must go around the footing; these support the weight of the building and anchor it.

Always install a gravel base; this provides a solid level place for concrete to rest on and facilitates drainage. Install over the gravel a plastic sheet; this will act as a vapor barrier. Make the floor at least 4 inches thick and reinforce it with steel mesh. Be sure the ground is absolutely level or concrete may crack eventually. Use thicker foundations (footings) where there is excessive weight, such as around the building walls.

In this greenhouse glass custom made skylights are used to provide light for plants. Skylight framing can be seen at upper right. (*Photo by author*).

For a small area (5 X 10 feet), rent a power mixer and put in 1 part cement, 2 parts sand, and 2 parts gravel or aggregate. First put in the water, followed by the gravel and sand, finishing with the cement. Work quickly before drying sets in. Smooth the floor at one time.

For larger areas, buy ready-mixed concrete and have it delivered. A truck generally holds about 7 yards; the concrete is run from the chute of the truck directly into the site where you have the forms in place. *(Having concrete pumped up a hill or into inaccessible places is more expensive.)* Work fast, within a 30-minute period, or you will be charged overtime. Get two friends: one should guide the chute *(or the truck driver might do this);* you and the other friend should get the mix in place with floats and trowels. If concrete starts to set before you have finished the pour, you are in trouble, so keep working fast. As the concrete pours, poke sticks into the footings to be sure concrete gets to all voids in the trenches.

Screeding is distributing the concrete at a uniform level in the form area and is done with a screed board *(a 2 X 4 nailed to a 1 X 2 handle).* Wear rubber boots and push and pull the board to evenly distribute the concrete. Now, if you want to, tamp down the concrete. Run an expanded metal screen over the concrete to level the slab and bring water, sand, and cement to the surface. Use a 2 X 6 wooden board with a handle (a float) to further level the concrete. Work the level <u>lightly</u> over large areas while the concrete is still wet; do not dig it in.

Concrete pavers make an easy and economical flooring almost impervious to destruction. Further they are easily installed and water evaporating on concrete provides humidity in the greenhouse. (*Photo by Matthew Barr*).

A brick floor is always charming and adds beauty to a greenhouse. It is somewhat more expensive than concrete pavers but does make a durable greenhouse flooring. (*Photo by Matthew Barr*).

Be sure the handle is long enough to reach the middle of the area of the slab from the outer edge. Use the float again when the concrete is somewhat set or looks sugary, and work in wide sweeps to level the slab.

Steel troweling, the final step, seals and waterproofs the slab and get rid of minor defects. When the concrete has set, remove the forms. For a few days, especially if the weather is hot, cover the area with plastic or burlap and keep it sprinkled so it cures slowly; slow curing gives you a strong floor.

Brick

Concrete is an excellent flooring material, but brick too has its merits: it is always handsome, easy to install, and weathers beautifully with time. Like concrete, it resists stain. Brick costs more than concrete.

The best brick for the greenhouse floor is smooth-surfaced or rough-textured common brick. Use hard-burned rather than green brick; use dark red brick rather than salmon, which indicates and underburned process and less durability. Keep the brick damp but not wet when laying it.

Brick can be laid on a sand base, but it is better to install it on a concrete slab with mortar. Use a thin mortar for laying the brick, with a heavier cement and grout in the interstices. *(Dark-colored cement for grouting gives a more dramatic effect.)* If you have to cut a brick, use a cold chisel and a brick hammer for making irregular cuts and trimming. Cut a groove along one side of the brick with the chisel or hammer, and then give it a

final severing blow. Cut the brick on a solid level surface, such as a piece of wood. Smooth uneven edges by rubbing them with another brick.

Cinders, Gravel

Cinders or gravel can be used for an inexpensive greenhouse floor; water evaporates slowly on these materials to provide good humidity for plants. For lightweight structures such as A-frames and plastic covered designs on footings or piers, the cinder or gravel floor is excellent. To install such a floor, dig down 4 to 6 inches and level the area. Insert gravel, rake it in place and put in more gravel until it is flush with the excavation.

Many times earth floors are used in greenhouses but they do get muddy so it is wise to put down some cinders or gravel over the earth.

Wood Floors

Somewhat like decking, redwood floors can be used in greenhouses in temperate climates. The flooring is put in place with spaces between the boards so excess water can escape—of course, drafts and cold air can also enter through these spaces. Yet, the redwood floor is handsome and as mentioned if climate will allow it do give it some consideration. Precast concrete piers are usually used as footings for wood floor greenhouses.

A concrete slab floor was the first step in building this greenhouse. Concrete makes a durable floor that lasts for years. *(Photo by author).*

4 Greenhouse Design

Because the greenhouse is essentially for plants, you want a structure that admits ample light. But too much light can harm plants. An all-glass greenhouse is not necessary; most plants will grow beautifully under a roof that allows 30 percent natural light *(this roof can be pitched, hipped, skylighted, domed, and so on).* Let your imagination soar and get away from the stereotyped greenhouse.

The lean-to, L or U-shaped, and court or atrium greenhouses are the most popular designs, but there are other types of places for plants. The A-frame, the lath house, the square greenhouse, and so on are much cheaper to build, and they are easy to construct in, say, a weekend.

Attached Units

Lean-To

This is by far the most popular greenhouse design because it is simple to build, easy on the pocketbook, and looks good, whether adjoining a kitchen, a dining room, or a bedroom. The lean-to uses one wall of the house and is a three-sided structure with a pitched roof. It can assume many designs, but generally it should match the character of the house so it looks like it belongs there rather than an attached afterthought. For example, if your house is rustic, design the greenhouse so it too has a rustic look:

heavy beams and thatched walls. If the home is more contemporary, stay with simple clean lines, using finished redwood or aluminum skeletons. Use some structural element of the main house—a post or mouldings—in the greenhouse to tie together the two and create a pleasing appearance.

The lean-to requires doors that enter to the main house. These can be inexpensive aluminum sliding doors or wooden doors. Be sure that door openings are wide; narrow doors make for a confining look, so use at least a 3 foot wide, 6 inch thick wooden door or 6 foot wide sliding doors.

The floor of the lean-to should be of a stain-resistant (to water) material like concrete or brick, not wood. Tile is expensive, and concrete generally looks institutional. However, a concrete aggregate floor or one with a wood-grid pattern will make the floor more charming and suitable to the home interior.

The most important consideration is the joint where the roof of the lean-to attaches to the house wall. This must be prepared carefully so leaks do not develop. Remove the siding on the existing house, insert metal flashing to avoid leaks, and then replace the siding. It is best to hire a professional roofer to make sure this is done properly.

The lean-to roof should be partially glass or have glass domes. For the average 16 X 20 greenhouse, allow four 37- X 37-inch

domes or, if using glass, 30 percent of the square footage. For example, if you have 320 square feet of roofing, 96 square feet of that will be glass. A glass skylight can be used, but it will be expensive. Also consider 1/4-inch plexiglass, which is easy to install, comes in sheets you can cut yourself *(but it will not cut you),* is easy to work with, and of course will not break if there is a hailstorm.

Converted Porch

By using the lean-to principle, many people have successfully converted porches and patios into splendid greenhouses. The floor is generally existing—for a patio, usually concrete or brick; if a porch, wood or sometimes concrete. The construction is relatively easy, as for a lean-to.

Use post and beam construction and sloped roofs; the slope allows water to drain off. The roof may be tar and gravel with plastic domes or metal skylights. There are a variety of designs you can use; it all depends on your budget and imagination.

Court (atrium)

This style is more commonly called an atrium—an open-to-the-sky area in the center of the house. Once roofed over it can become a charming greenhouse, an actual part of the home, and a definite asset because it is visible from most rooms and thus presents a very pleasant view. The atrium

ATTACHED GREENHOUSE

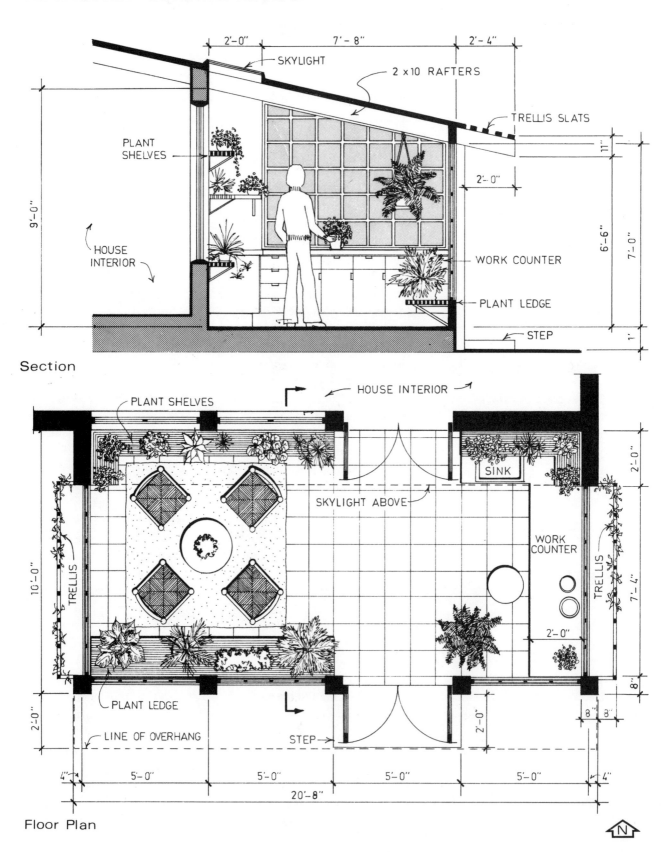

2'-0" 7'-8" 2'-4"

SKYLIGHT

2 x 10 RAFTERS

TRELLIS SLATS

PLANT SHELVES

11"

2'-0"

9'-0"

HOUSE INTERIOR

6'-6"

7'-0"

WORK COUNTER

PLANT LEDGE

STEP

1'

Section

HOUSE INTERIOR

PLANT SHELVES

SINK

SKYLIGHT ABOVE

2'-0"

10'-0"

TRELLIS

WORK COUNTER

TRELLIS

7'-4"

2'-0"

8"

2'-0"

PLANT LEDGE

LINE OF OVERHANG

STEP

8" 8"

4" 5'-0" 5'-0" 5'-0" 5'-0" 4"

20'-8"

Floor Plan

N

ATTACHED GREENHOUSE

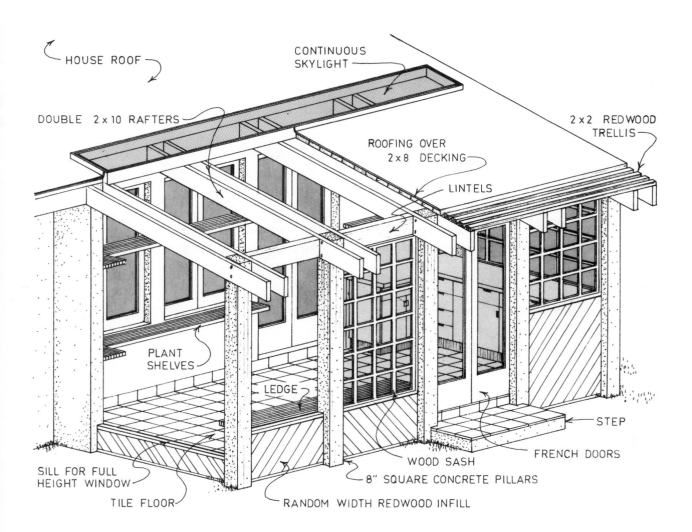

HOUSE ROOF

CONTINUOUS SKYLIGHT

DOUBLE 2 x 10 RAFTERS

2 x 2 REDWOOD TRELLIS

ROOFING OVER 2 x 8 DECKING

LINTELS

PLANT SHELVES

LEDGE

STEP

FRENCH DOORS

WOOD SASH

8" SQUARE CONCRETE PILLARS

SILL FOR FULL HEIGHT WINDOW

TILE FLOOR

RANDOM WIDTH REDWOOD INFILL

ROOF
CONTINUATION OF HOUSE ROOF, DOUBLE 2 x 10 RAFTERS BOLTED TO PILLARS, 2 x 8 DECKING W/ ROOFING ABOVE, 2 x 2 REDWOOD SLAT TRELLIS AT OVERHANG

SKYLIGHT
2' WIDE CONTINUOUS WIRE GLASS SKYLIGHT AT LINE OF HOUSE WALL, WOOD FRAMED

STRUCTURE
8" SQUARE REINFORCED CONCRETE PILLARS, 4 x 8 LINTELS ABOVE DOORS & WINDOWS, WOOD FRAME WALLS BELOW, W/ RANDOM WIDTH, DIAGONAL REDWOOD SIDING, WALLS ADJACENT TO HOUSE ARE A CONTINUATION OF THE HOUSE STRUCTURE

FLOOR & STEP
REINFORCED CONCRETE, INCLUDING FOOTINGS, WALL BASE & FLOOR TILED

WINDOWS
VARYING HEIGHTS, WOOD FRAMED W/ OPERABLE WOOD SASH

DOORS
WOOD FRAMED DOUBLE FRENCH DOORS, ALSO INTO HOUSE INTERIOR

WORK COUNTER
PLYWOOD CABINETS, W/ PLASTIC LAMINATE COUNTERTOP & STAINLESS STEEL SINK

PLANT SHELVES & LEDGE
1 x 2 REDWOOD SLATS ON STEEL BRACKETS, PLANT LEDGE ATTACHED TO WINDOW SILL

NOTE:
FOR SUMMER SOLAR PROTECTION ON EAST & WEST SIDES, TRAIN DECIDUOUS VINES ON RED-WOOD TRELLISES - ATTACH 1' AWAY FROM SIDE WINDOWS

CONVERTING A PORCH

Interior View

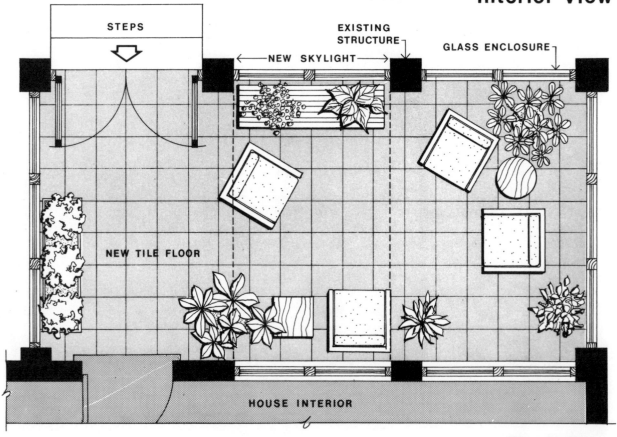

STEPS

EXISTING
STRUCTURE

NEW SKYLIGHT

GLASS ENCLOSURE

NEW TILE FLOOR

HOUSE INTERIOR

Floor Plan

greenhouse should always be in scale with the house.

Because the house walls are used as the basis for the court greenhouse, all you have to do is enclose the ceiling. Use glass skylights, or domes, or try translucent acrylic sheets of corrugated plastic on a wood frame.

Air circulation does not have to be a problem even though this greenhouse is in the center of the home. Use jalousie windows, small fans, and upper vents for ventilation. Light in the atrium greenhouse will not be the best because of the walled enclosure, but many kinds of plants can thrive in such light.

L- or U-shaped Greenhouse

This design offers the home owner many advantages because it means building only one or two walls and using house walls as the

Inside a lean-to greenhouse you can see the basic construction using the house wall as one wall and a dome to admit natural light. Lean-to construction is relatively simple and porches or patios as well can be converted to a greenhouse. (*Photo by Clark Photo Graphics*).

This atrium type greenhouse is elaborate and lovely and houses many, many plants as well as a seating area for people. It is a desirable addition to the home. (*Photo by Matthew Barr*).

47

L-SHAPED GREENHOUSE

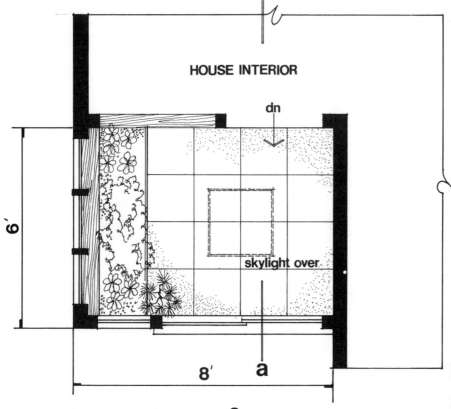

HOUSE INTERIOR

dn

skylight over

6'

8'

a

Floor Plan

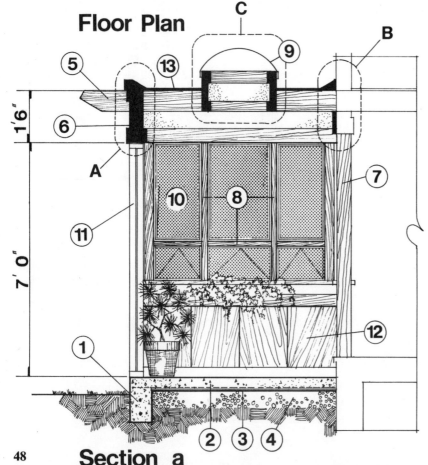

C

B

A

⑤

⑬

⑨

⑥

1'6"

⑩

⑧

⑦

⑪

7'0"

①

② ③ ④

⑫

Section a

Materials

FOUNDATIONS
① REINFORCED CONCRETE

FLOOR
② CONCRETE
③ VAPOR BARRIER
④ GRAVEL

STRUCTURE
⑤ BEAMS 7-2×8s at 8'
⑥ HEADER 2-2×10s at 8'
⑦ POST 1-4×4 at 7'
⑧ MULLIONS 3-2×6s at 5'

WINDOW WALL
⑨ SKYLIGHT
⑩ GLASS
⑪ SLIDING GLASS DOOR
   7'0"H × 5'0"W

CABINETS
⑫ PLYWOOD - 12 sq. ft.

ROOF
⑬ TAR & GRAVEL

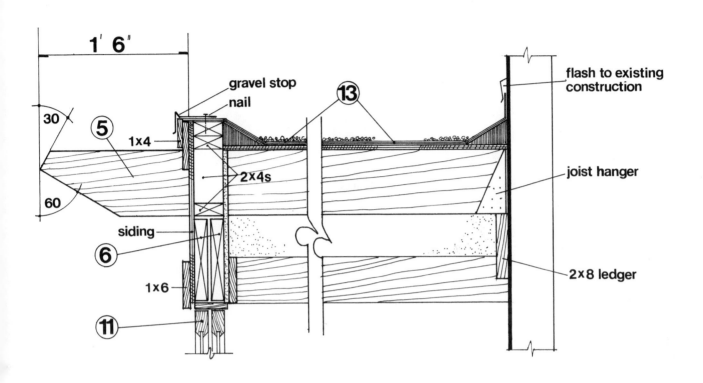

1' 6"

gravel stop

nail

⑬

30

⑤

1x4

2x4s

flash to existing construction

joist hanger

60

siding

⑥

2x8 ledger

1x6

⑪

A
Details

B

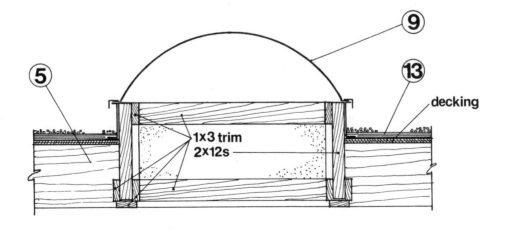

⑨

⑤

⑬

decking

1x3 trim

2x12s

Detail C

GALLERY GREENHOUSE

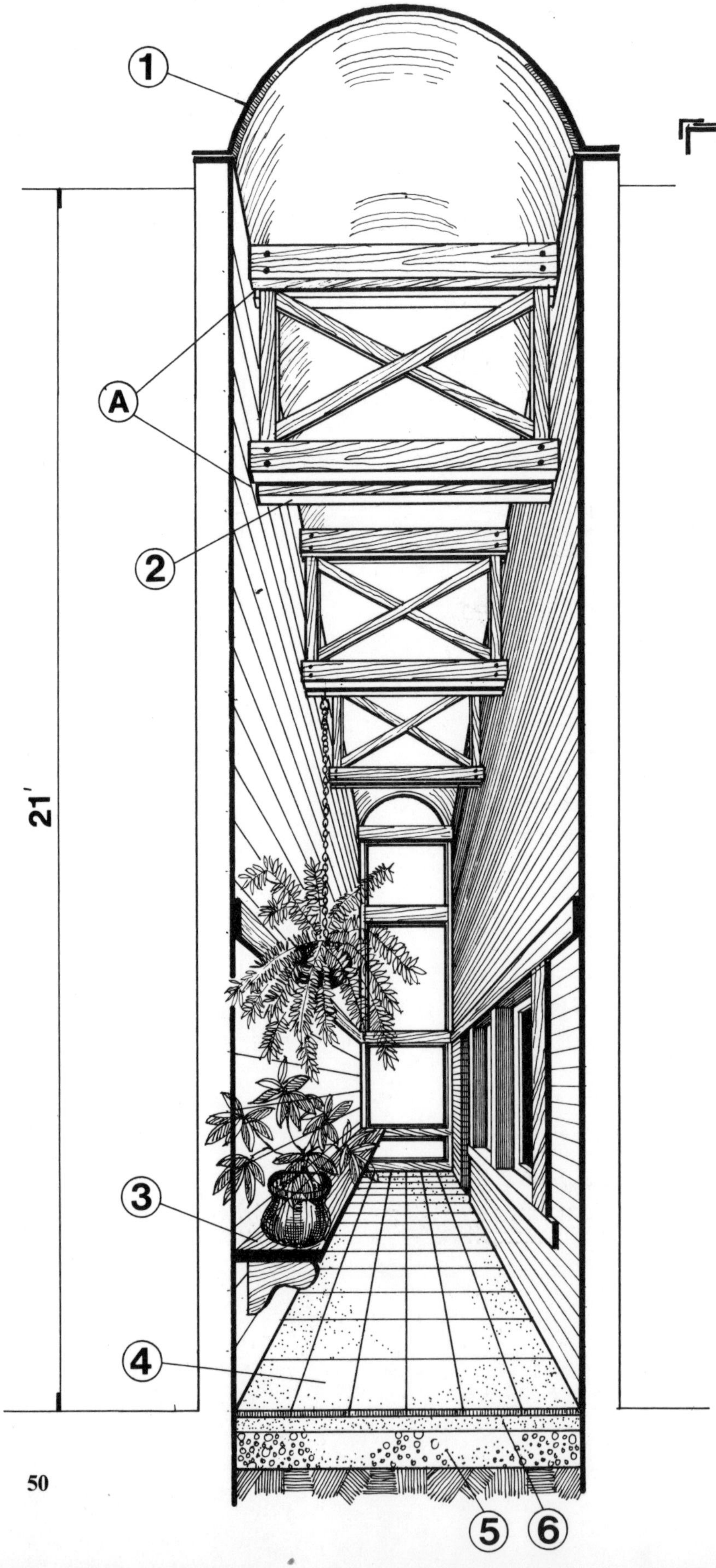

① — A ②

21′

③

④

⑤ ⑥

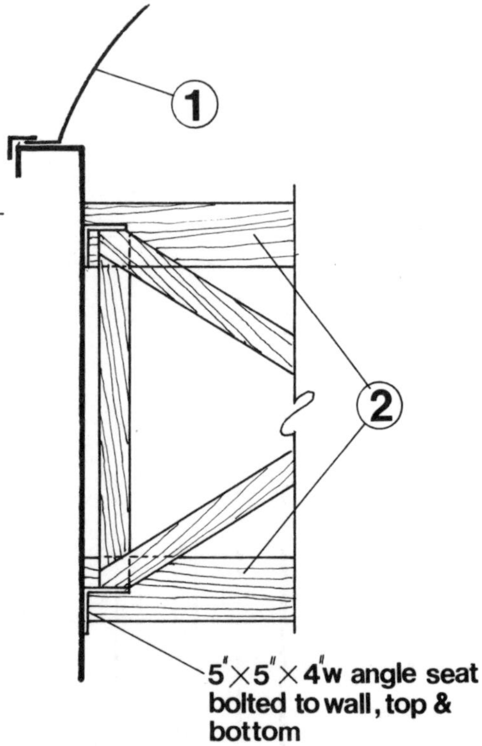

1 — ②

5′×5″×4′w angle seat
bolted to wall, top &
bottom

Detail A

Materials

① BARREL VAULT SKYLIGHT
6′wide x 16′ long

② WOOD TRUSSES (3)
CHORDS 12-2x8s at 6′
WEBS 9-1x4s at 8′
6- 2x4s at 4′

③ POTTING BENCH
two 3/4″ x 8′ plywood

④ QUARRY TILE
100 sq. ft.

⑤ GRAVEL

⑥ SAND

Interior View

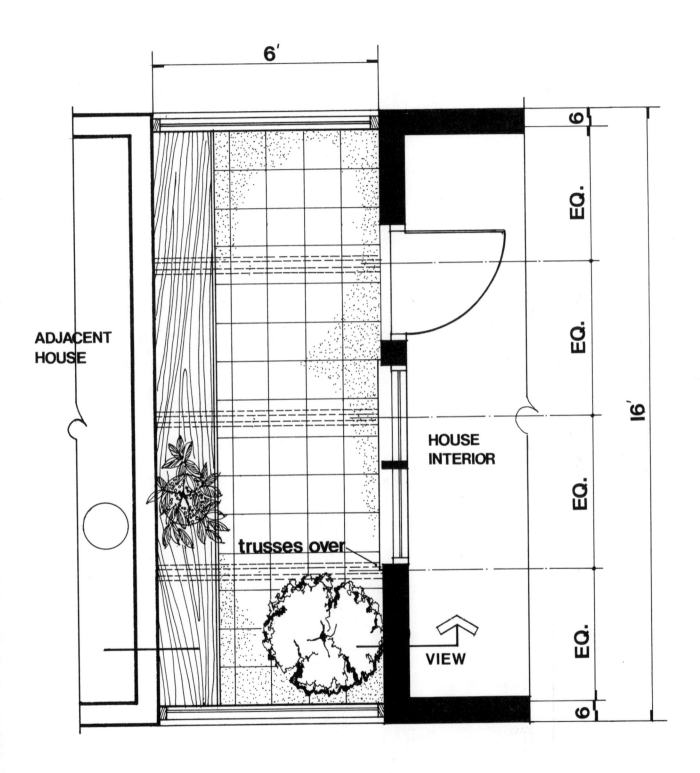

6'

6

EQ.

EQ.

ADJACENT
HOUSE

HOUSE
INTERIOR

EQ.

16'

trusses over

EQ.

VIEW

6

Floor Plan

WINDOW GREENHOUSE

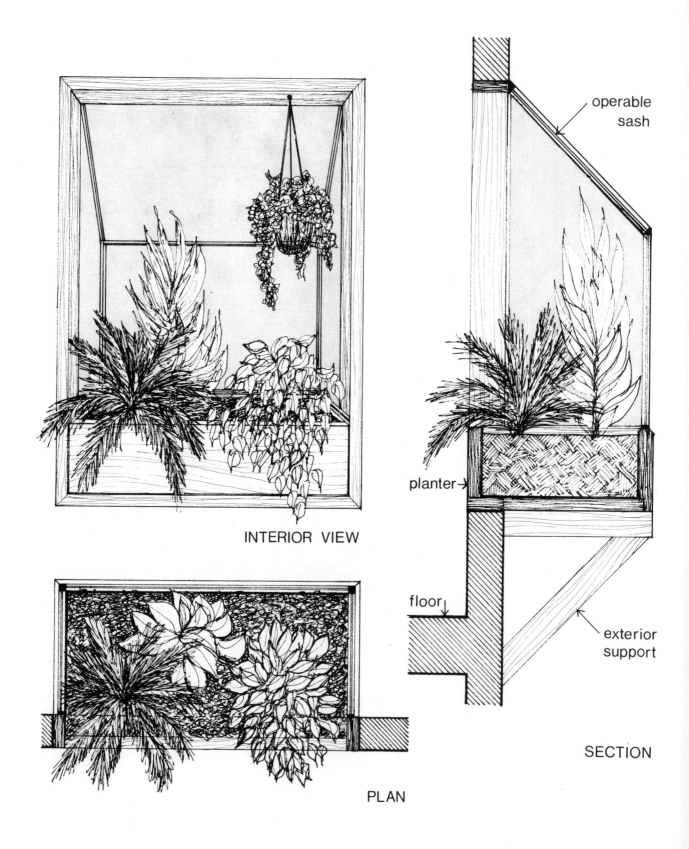

INTERIOR VIEW

PLAN

operable sash

planter

floor

exterior support

SECTION

other supporting members of the greenhouse. Also, the addition of only one or two walls and a roof add space to the main house and make it appear visually larger. Such a structure is shaded by the house from wind and, in some cases, hot sun.

The L or U shape can be as narrow as 6 feet and still lend a pleasing area that is in scale with most average-sized homes. It provides two areas of greenery: one as a display and one side as a working greenhouse. Also, the wrap-around effect of such an enclosure can enhance the appearance of the house.

The construction of these greenhouses is even simpler than for the lean-to. It follows the same rules but requires less work and materials. The L- or U-shaped greenhouse is indeed a perfect way to add a place for plants to the home.

Window Greenhouse

For the apartment dweller or someone with little space, a window greenhouse opens the door to gardening. In these small greeneries it is possible to grow a host of plants, including vegetables, herbs, and house plants, and you can also sow seeds of various plants.

Prefabricated window greenhouses to fit different-sized windows are available; manufacturers will send details *(see back of book)*. These greenhouses are fine for some windows, but many apartments and homes do not have the standard double-hung windows. This is where the homemade window greenhouse can be a blessing: you can create your own design and arrangement that will accommodate almost any window opening.

Although the prefabricated unit is available only in metal, the unit you make should be built with wood because the total picture is far more handsome than the stereotyped packaged unit. This kind of window greenhouse adds infinite charm to a kitchen or dining room and truly brings the outdoors indoors. It acts both as a place for plants and as a decorative piece.

BUILDING THE WOODEN
WINDOW GREENHOUSE

The prefabricated metal unit is simple to install on an existing window once the window itself has been removed. Simply put mouldings in place, and as outlined in the instruction sheet included with packages, install shelves.

The homemade unit will require a sketch; the basic building materials, such as wood and glass and a concrete shelf, are shown in the photograph. The wooden window greenhouse should be designed so the glass is at an angle to catch as much sun as possible and to look more dramatic and appealing.

Redwood is the framing material; it should be painted for looks and durability. Construct windows with one-piece moullions, each rabbeted to accept glass panes. Forms for the concrete base are necessary, and generally some bracing is required at the bottom of the cement shelf, not an altogether difficult project.

A homemade window greenhouse greatly enhances the scene and provides ample space for dozens of plants. It is a joy to have these bright plants as part of your home in winter mornings and construction of a window greenhouse is not expensive. (*Photo by Max Eckert*).

LOFT GREENHOUSE

FLOOR PLANS

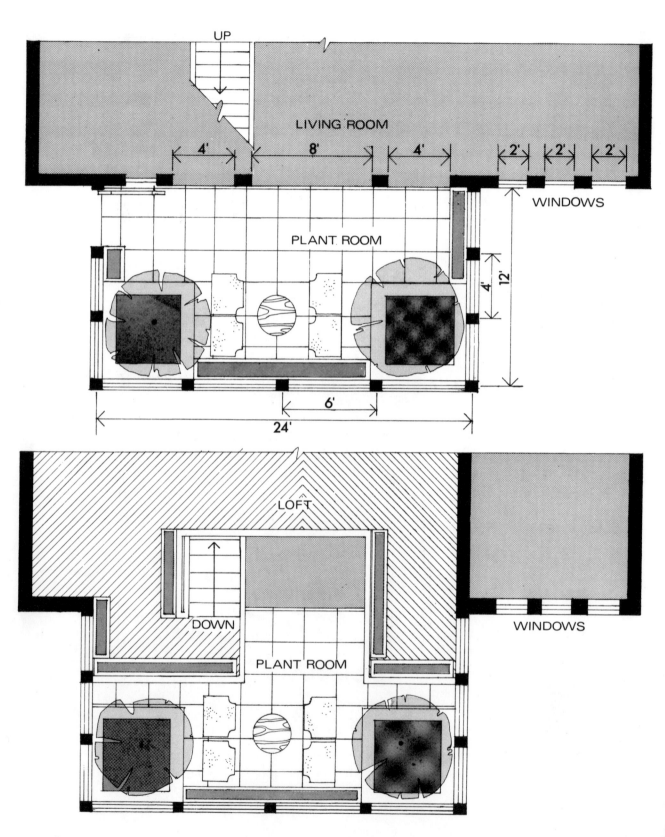

UP

LIVING ROOM

4'   8'   4'   2' 2' 2'

WINDOWS

PLANT ROOM

12'

4'

6'

24'

LOFT

DOWN

WINDOWS

PLANT ROOM

LOFT GREENHOUSE

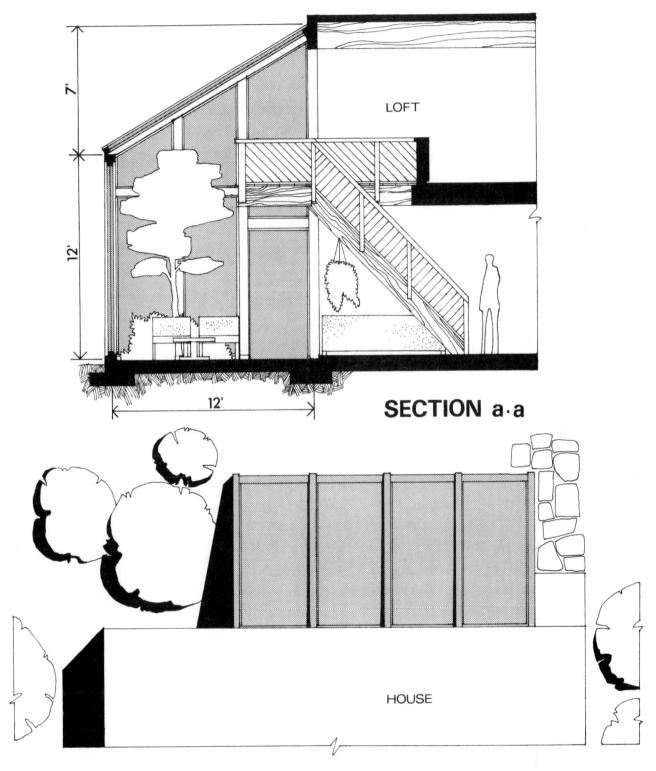

7'

12'

12'

LOFT

SECTION a·a

HOUSE

SITE PLAN

LOFT GREENHOUSE

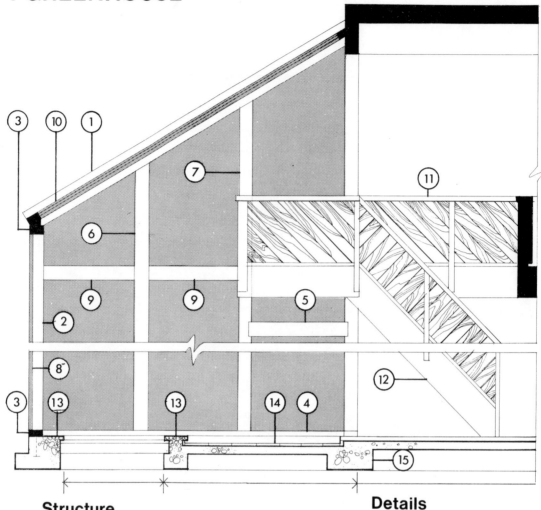

Structure

① RAFTERS   5-6X10sX15
② POSTS   5-6X6sX12
③ PLATES   2-4X6X24

Windows

⑧ WINDOW   GLASS ON WOOD

Roof

⑩ STEEL-FRAMED WIRED GLASS

Loft

⑪ RAILING   2X6s & 4s, REDWOOD
    PLANKING

Foundation   Floor

⑬ EXPOSED AGGREGATE
⑭ QUARRY TILE

Details

④ 2-4X6s X 12
⑤ HEADERS   4 X 8
⑥ 2-6 X 6s X 15
⑦ 2-6 X 6s X 17

⑨ FRAMING   4X6

⑫ LAMINATED WOOD

⑮ REINFORCED CONCRETE

Materials

Greenhouses in The Air

Greenhouses on upper levels—garage roofs, on car-ports or rooms—are becoming popular because they are a separate entity and look dramatic. Most people think of the upper greenhouse as a lean-to but it can be a separate structure on a roof or on footings-and-posts *(at building supply houses)*.

Make sure the design of the upstairs greenhouse is in character with the architecture of the adjoining building. Do not just add a box because it will always look like just a box! If it is on top of a room be sure the existing roof can take the extra weight *(an architect can advise you)*. In such cases, flooring and drainage facilities must be near perfect so there is absolutely no leakage. A second-floor greenhouse above a carport or on piers and footings, as mentioned, is thus more ideal because if some leakage does occur there is no harm.

The second floor greenhouse is generally of frame construction with a pitched roof. Posts can be 6 X 6, beams 6 X 8, and sills, 2 X 6. A suitable floor—concrete, decking, if weather permits—can be used. The roof can be partially wire glass or glass and wood; walls can be wood and glass also.

Detached Units

A-Frame

The A-frame looks good, is sensible because the triangle is the strongest form, can be put together in a day even by the person who is not too terribly handy with tools, and can be converted into a permanent building if and when necessary. Use redwood framing,

This A-frame skeleton made of redwood can easily be converted into a handsome greenhouse. It needs an outer skin which may be glass or plastic, and doors. (*Photo courtesy California Redwood Association*).

A dome greenhouse is a popular one because it utilizes every inch of space and there is ample room for plants. There are many kinds of domes that could be adaptable to greenhouse structures. (*Photo courtesy Redwood Domes*).

ROOF-TOP GREENHOUSE

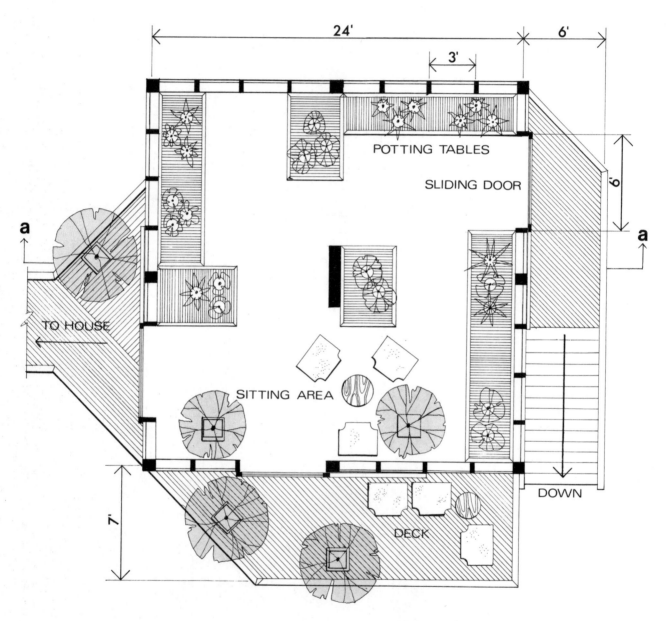

24'

6'

3'

POTTING TABLES

SLIDING DOOR

6'

a

a

TO HOUSE

DOWN

SITTING AREA

7'

DECK

Floor Plan

ROOF-TOP GREENHOUSE

SECTION a-a

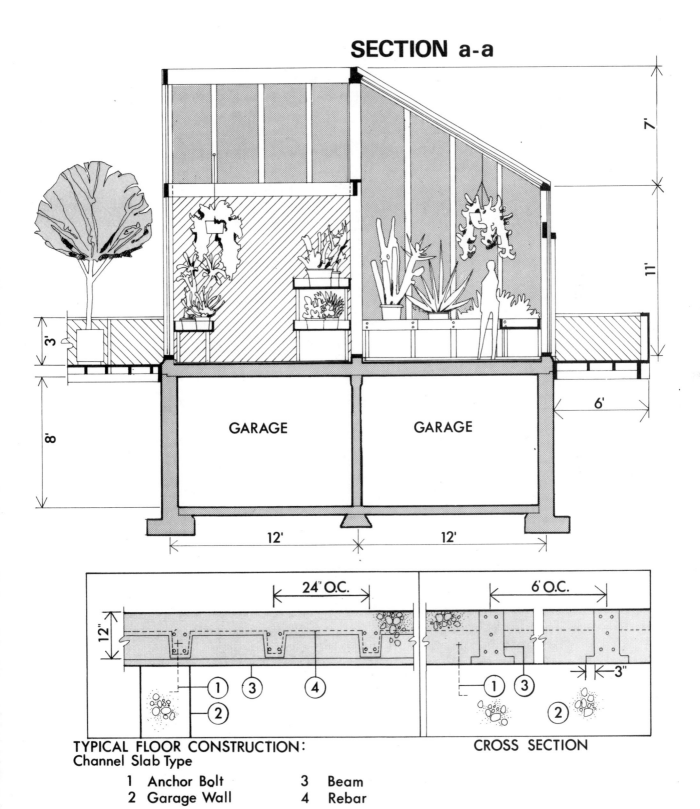

7'

11'

3'

8'

6'

GARAGE

GARAGE

12'

12'

24" O.C.

6' O.C.

12"

3"

① ③ ④

② ③

① ③

②

TYPICAL FLOOR CONSTRUCTION:
Channel Slab Type

1   Anchor Bolt   3   Beam
2   Garage Wall   4   Rebar

CROSS SECTION

LOW COST GREENHOUSE

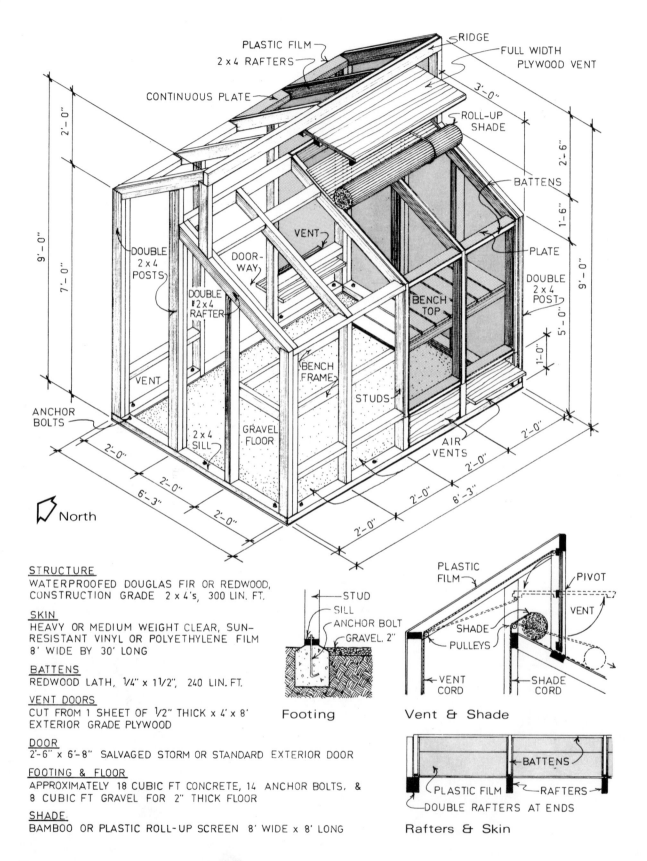

PLASTIC FILM
2 x 4 RAFTERS
RIDGE
FULL WIDTH PLYWOOD VENT
CONTINUOUS PLATE
3'-0"
ROLL-UP SHADE
2'-0"
7'-0"
9'-0"
DOUBLE 2 x 4 POSTS
DOOR-WAY
VENT
2'-6"
1'-6"
BATTENS
DOUBLE 2 x 4 RAFTER
PLATE
9'-0"
BENCH TOP
DOUBLE 2 x 4 POST
VENT
5'-0"
BENCH FRAME
STUDS
1'-0"
ANCHOR BOLTS
2 x 4 SILL
GRAVEL FLOOR
AIR VENTS
2'-0"
2'-0"
2'-0"
2'-0"
2'-0"
6'-3"
2'-0"
8'-3"
2'-0"

North

STRUCTURE
WATERPROOFED DOUGLAS FIR OR REDWOOD,
CONSTRUCTION GRADE 2 x 4's, 300 LIN. FT.

SKIN
HEAVY OR MEDIUM WEIGHT CLEAR, SUN-
RESISTANT VINYL OR POLYETHYLENE FILM
8' WIDE BY 30' LONG

BATTENS
REDWOOD LATH, 1/4" x 1 1/2", 240 LIN. FT.

VENT DOORS
CUT FROM 1 SHEET OF 1/2" THICK x 4' x 8'
EXTERIOR GRADE PLYWOOD

DOOR
2'-6" x 6'-8" SALVAGED STORM OR STANDARD EXTERIOR DOOR

FOOTING & FLOOR
APPROXIMATELY 18 CUBIC FT CONCRETE, 14 ANCHOR BOLTS, &
8 CUBIC FT GRAVEL FOR 2" THICK FLOOR

SHADE
BAMBOO OR PLASTIC ROLL-UP SCREEN 8' WIDE x 8' LONG

STUD
SILL
ANCHOR BOLT
GRAVEL, 2"

Footing

PLASTIC FILM
PIVOT
VENT
SHADE
PULLEYS
VENT CORD
SHADE CORD

Vent & Shade

BATTENS
PLASTIC FILM
RAFTERS
DOUBLE RAFTERS AT ENDS

Rafters & Skin

60

A-FRAME GREENHOUSE

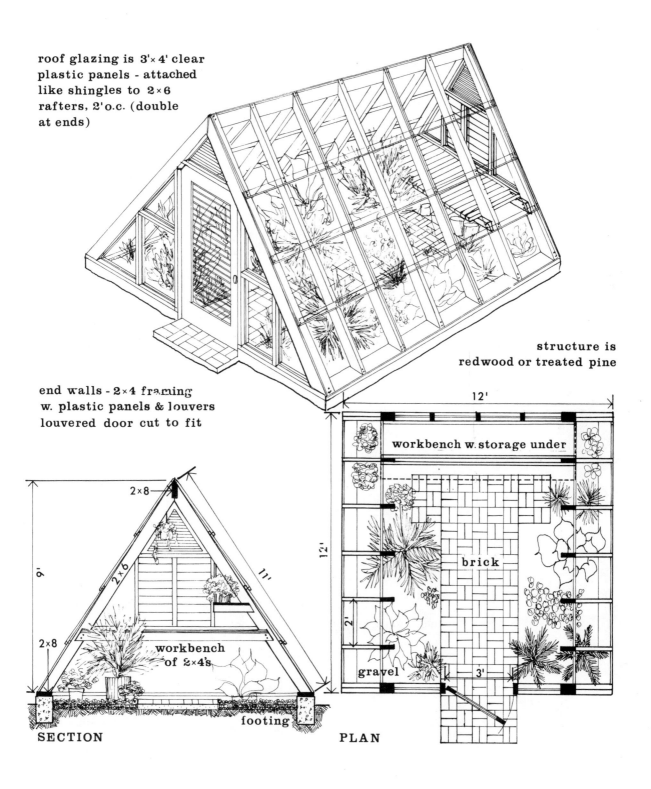

roof glazing is 3'× 4' clear
plastic panels - attached
like shingles to 2×6
rafters, 2'o.c. (double
at ends)

structure is
redwood or treated pine

end walls - 2×4 framing
w. plastic panels & louvers
louvered door cut to fit

2×8

2×6

9'

11'

2×8

workbench
of 2×4's

footing

SECTION

12'

workbench w. storage under

brick

12'

2'

gravel

3'

PLAN

Arched greenhouse design affords ample room for plants, is easy to build and inexpensive. This one is glazed with corrugated fiberglas and comes from the Gothic Arch Greenhouse Company as a prefabricated kit.

This steel and fiberglas greenhouse also uses the arch design and comes in three lengths. It is a very functional durable unit and is manufactured by Environmental Dynamics Company.

with 2- X 4-foot rafters covered with flexible or rigid plastic. Dig two parallel trenches 12 inches deep and 12 inches wide. Nail four 2 X 12 rafters to a 1 X 10 ridge and then raise the skeleton, supporting it by temporarily bracing it in the ground. Now nail the other rafters to the ridge and fashion bridging between the rafters. Put the 2 X 4 and 2 X 2 cross braces in place between opposite rafters. At one end put in a frame for a door, and allow space for ventilating fans in two areas.

For the footing pour a mixture of 1 part cement, 3 parts gravel, and 2 parts sand into the trench around the rafters. Do not remove the braces until the concrete is thoroughly set. Next, saw cut fiberglas panels to fit the wooden skeleton and nail them to the frame, allowing one corrugation overlap between them. If you use flat material, allow a 2-inch overlap. To weatherproof the ceiling, apply mastic between the panels before nailing them in place *(use aluminum nails to prevent rust)*. The floor can be gravel or soil or bricks laid in sand.

The A-frame provides ample ceiling height for tall plants. For an ideal arrangement use one side for benches, the other for floor plants. Suspend any hanging plants from rafters, using wire or chain.

Dome Greenhouse

The dome adapts quite well to greenhouse design. There are many kinds of domes, including geodisic, hexagonal, and polyhedrene. The dome is inexpensive to build, but not as easy for the average person to construct as the A-frame. It is an ideal place for plants because its hemispherical shape provides plants with maximum light.

It also utilizes every inch of space; and in a dome greenhouse there is ample ceiling height for tall plants. The fallacy of the dome as a greenhouse *(if there is one)* is that it admits too much light because it generally is an all-glass or plastic structure; plants will burn. Heating in winter is difficult, and in summer domes can get very hot. Still, this is a pleasing, inexpensive structure, and you can eliminate some glass areas by using plywood or other opaque materials.

Making your own dome greenhouse will take time and patience and some experience in carpentry, but it is not impossible. A good size for a beginner is a structure 14 feet in diameter; for anything larger you definitely would need help. You can also buy prefabricated dome greenhouses *(and the ones I have seen are quite handsome)* with all the parts; these are relatively easy to put together. *(See supply list at end of book).* Again, let me say that instead of using all glass, substitute other materials.

Because there are so many types of domes, it is important to familiarize yourself with domes before starting a design. We show some basic dome construction; for further reading refer to the Dome Builder's Handbook, edited by John Prenis, *(Running Press, Philadelphia, Pa.).*

Arched Greenhouse

The shape of this rather clean, neat greenhouse is conducive to growing many plants, tall and small. There is ample length and

This lath house was built for less than $50 and is a fine temporary place for plants. Again, it can always be glazed later with suitable weathertight materials. (*Photo by Clark Photo Graphics*).

A simple rectangular greenhouse is a sanctuary for plants—and you too. Of wood, plastic, and glass, this is a detached unit in a yard. (*Photo by Matthew Barr*).

63

DOME GREENHOUSE

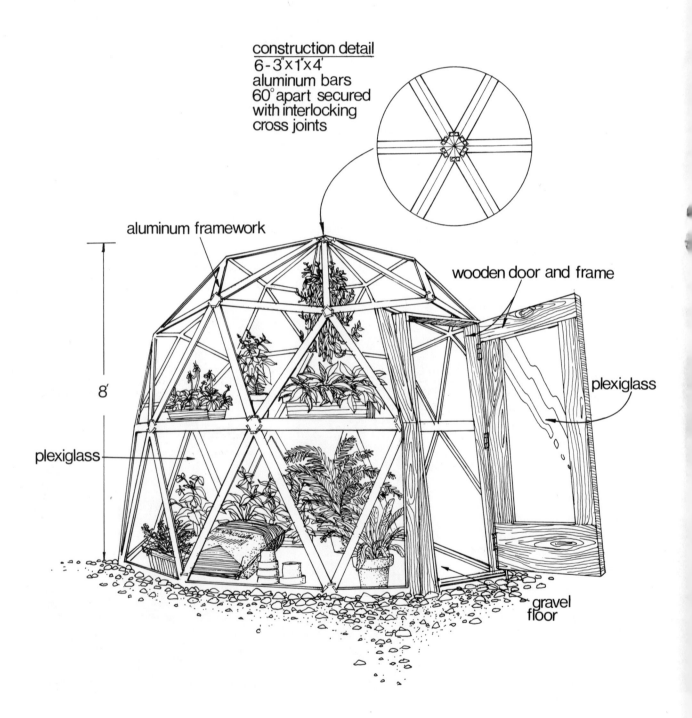

construction detail
6 - 3"x 1"x 4'
aluminum bars
60° apart secured
with interlocking
cross joints

aluminum framework

wooden door and frame

plexiglass

8'

plexiglass

gravel
floor

This artificial light greenery is indeed handsome and an ideal answer for a place for plants when there is no space outdoors. (*Photo by Hedrich Blessing*).

ARCHED GREENHOUSE

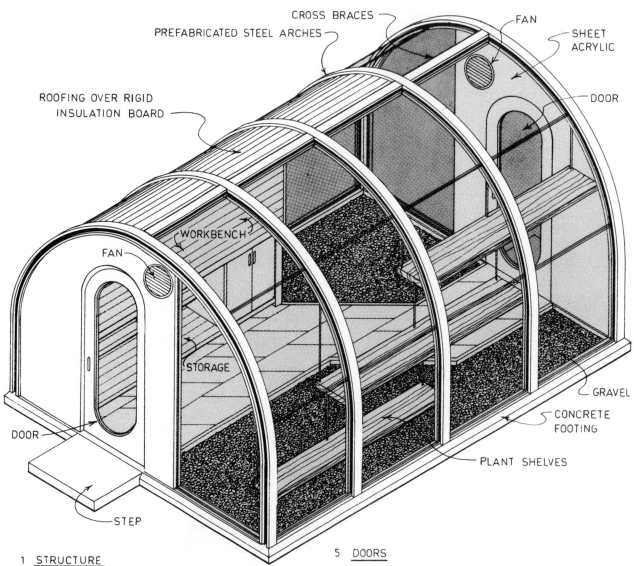

CROSS BRACES

PREFABRICATED STEEL ARCHES

FAN

SHEET ACRYLIC

ROOFING OVER RIGID INSULATION BOARD

DOOR

WORKBENCH

FAN

STORAGE

DOOR

STEP

GRAVEL

CONCRETE FOOTING

PLANT SHELVES

1 STRUCTURE

PREFABRICATED STEEL I-BEAM ARCHES, 5–27'
LONG x 4" SQ., 6' RADIUS SEMICIRCLE, SET INTO
CONCRETE FOOTING   I-BEAM BRACES AT TOP

2 OPAQUE ROOF & WALLS

3" THICK RIGID INSULATION BOARD, WATERPROOFED,
ROOFING OVER ARCHED SURFACES

3 TRANSPARENT ROOF & WALLS

$\frac{1}{8}$" SHEET ACRYLIC PLASTIC IN ALUMINUM FRAMES

4 FLOOR

CONCRETE TILES IN REDWOOD FRAMING & GRAVEL
OVER SOIL, CONCRETE STEPS AT DOORS

5 DOORS

3' x 7', PLYWOOD W/SHEET ACRYLIC WINDOWS

6 WORK/STORAGE UNIT

REDWOOD WORKBENCH & SHELVES, REDWOOD
PLYWOOD STORAGE CABINET

7 PLANT SHELVES

REDWOOD, 8' LONG, VARYING WIDTHS, SUSPENDED
BY STEEL RODS FROM ARCHES

NOTE:

SPACE IS VENTED BY FANS BUILT INTO END WALLS,
& HEATED WITH A PORTABLE SPACE HEATER

ARCHED GREENHOUSE

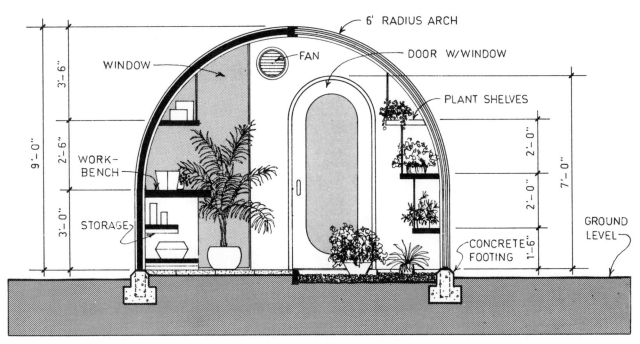

6' RADIUS ARCH

FAN

DOOR W/WINDOW

WINDOW

PLANT SHELVES

3'-6"

2'-6"

9'-0"

WORK-
BENCH

2'-0"

2'-0"

7'-0"

3'-0"

STORAGE

CONCRETE
FOOTING

1'-6"

GROUND
LEVEL

Section

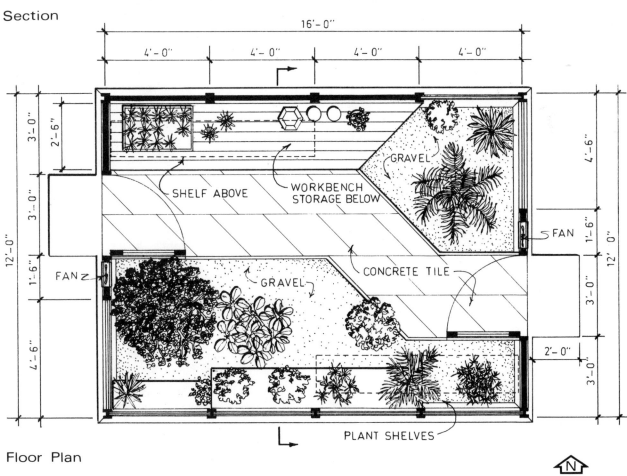

16'-0"

4'-0"   4'-0"   4'-0"   4'-0"

3'-0"

2'-6"

GRAVEL

SHELF ABOVE

4'-6"

WORKBENCH
STORAGE BELOW

3'-0"

FAN

12'-0"

1'-6"

FAN

GRAVEL

CONCRETE TILE

12'-0"

3'-0"

2'-0"

4'-6"

3'-0"

PLANT SHELVES

Floor Plan

N

height, and the round lines are more in keeping with the human shape. It is strong, and new building materials make the arched greenhouse very feasible for the amateur carpenter.

You can also buy a fine prefabricated arch shape greenhouse made of kiln dried heart redwood glazed in fiberglas. The unit lacks the handcrafted look but it is certainly fine for plants and as mentioned previously you can add your own personal touches to give it some charm.

Whether you make your own arch greenhouse with I-beams or buy a prefab, remember that these are totally enclosed structures and fans will be necessary to ensure fresh air circulation. These can be built into end walls. A portable space heater can be used for heating. This is a totally utilitarian structure, fine for plants and not costly. Again, I must say its appearance is somewhat alien to the natural scene but certainly not objectionable, and such a structure properly built can last a very long time.

Lath House

Too often this structure is of haphazard design and unattractive. Yet with some planning it can be a desirable functional feature in the landscape. It can be made of open slats to create a pleasing design or trellis work, which is indeed handsome. The lath house reduces the intensity of the sun, providing coolness within. The alternating sun and shade provides almost ideal conditions for plants.

The size and shape of the enclosure is determined by the site; a good size is 10 X 12 feet. The width of a single lath is generally

the best space for maximum sun control, but a trellis ceiling (laths crossing) is acceptable too and more handsome. Construct the house with a sloping roof so rain runs down the laths and plants are protected from dripping water.

Because this is a lightweight structure, footings can be commercial precast concrete piers. Use 2 X 4 redwood for the vertical members, spaced about 4 feet apart; for roof construction use 2 X 4 double beams. The lath house can be used without a covering as a temporary shelter, finished with fiberglas, or glazed with lightweight acrylic for a permanent place.

Square or Rectangular Greenhouse

This detached and inexpensive structure is easy to build in a weekend. Use corrugated or flat, rigid fiberglas sheets throughout and 2 X 4s with 2 X 6 rafters for framing. A sliding glass door works fine for an entrance. Select any color fiberglas you like, but the more neutral shades blend better with the landscape than very bright colors.

Use post and beam construction, with a redwood skeleton. Nail the fiberglas sheets in place with overlapping joints of 2 inches; use a plastic mastic between joints to ensure weatherproofing. Allow for an overhang; it makes the building look better. Pitch the roof slightly so water runs off. Because no windows are involved (there is no need for them), provide ventilation (fans and louvers).

For the floor, dig out 4 inches of soil, level the area of debris, and insert a bed of gravel. This

material will of course have to be replaced periodically, but it does supply good humidity in the greenhouse as water on it evaporates. The support for the greenhouse can be concrete piers at each corner because little weight is involved.

A variation of this kind of construction is shown in the drawing titled Low-Cost Greenhouse, where 2 X 4s are used almost exclusively throughout the structure—for rafters, posts, and beams. The frame is then covered with polyethylene film for a very inexpensive yet good-looking and functional greenhouse.

Artificial Light Greeneries

On several occasions I have seen apartment greenhouses that use artificial light. This is not a true greenhouse in the sense of the word; it is a nook, alcove, or small area that has been converted to a place to grow plants. Artificial light furnishes the necessary light plants need for growth.

The floor of the growing area must be tile, brick, or some other material impervious to water stain. Or it can be a galvanized metal pan filled with white gravel (very attractive). Potted plants can be put on pedestals or inverted pots, or small benches similar to greenhouse benches can be installed.

Track lighting is used on the ceiling; these systems are at electrical dealers under various trade names; for example, Power Trac by Halo Lighting, Lite Span by Lightolier Lighting. Bullet or canopy fixtures are attached to the track at any given point, and in-

LATH GREENHOUSE

all lumber is redwood or
treated pine

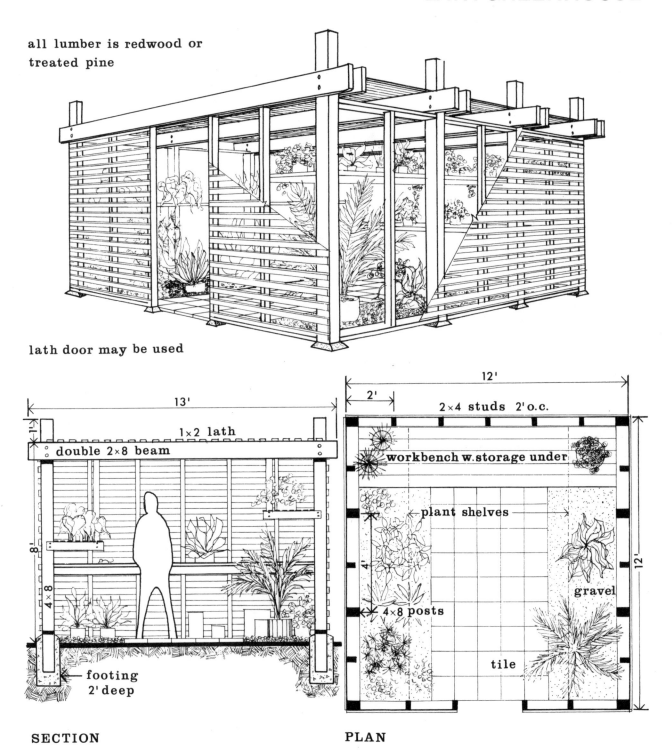

lath door may be used

13'

1×2 lath

double 2×8 beam

1"

8'

4×8

footing
2' deep

SECTION

12'

2'

2×4 studs 2'o.c.

workbench w. storage under

plant shelves

4'

4×8 posts

gravel

tile

12'

PLAN

SQUARE GREENHOUSE

SECTION a·a & FLOOR PLAN

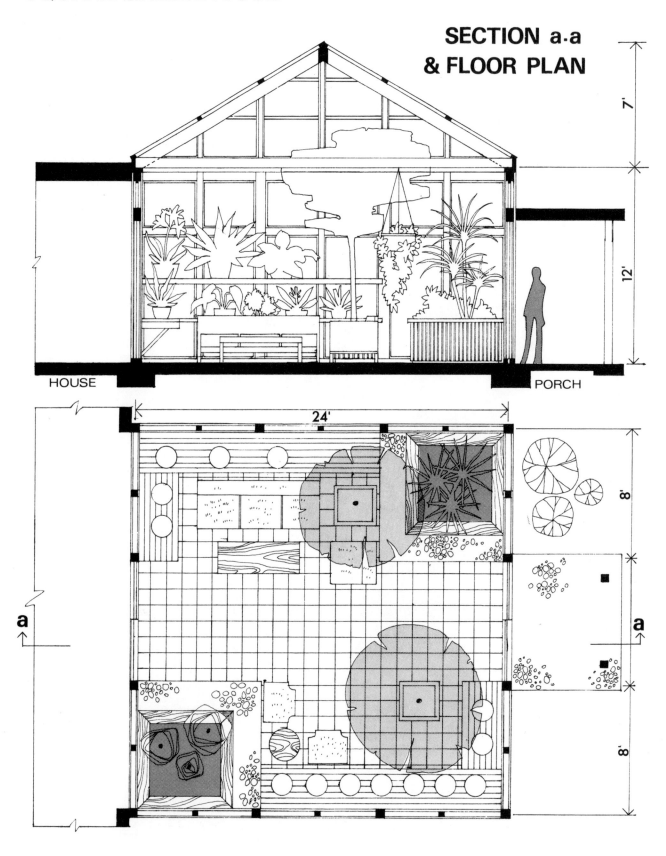

7'

12'

HOUSE

PORCH

24'

8'

8'

a

a

SQUARE GREENHOUSE

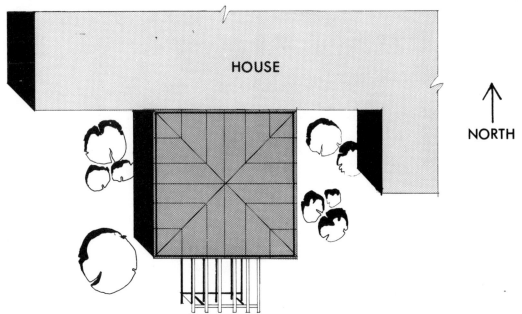

HOUSE

↑
NORTH

SITE PLAN

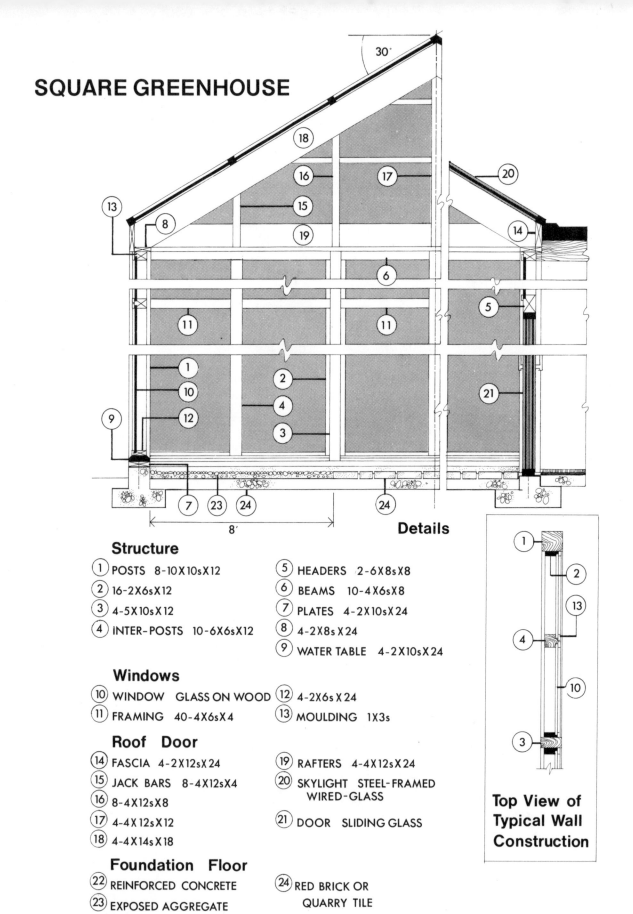

SQUARE GREENHOUSE

30°

Details

Structure

1. POSTS 8-10X10sX12
2. 16-2X6sX12
3. 4-5X10sX12
4. INTER-POSTS 10-6X6sX12
5. HEADERS 2-6X8sX8
6. BEAMS 10-4X6sX8
7. PLATES 4-2X10sX24
8. 4-2X8sX24
9. WATER TABLE 4-2X10sX24

Windows

10. WINDOW GLASS ON WOOD
11. FRAMING 40-4X6sX4
12. 4-2X6sX24
13. MOULDING 1X3s

Roof Door

14. FASCIA 4-2X12sX24
15. JACK BARS 8-4X12sX4
16. 8-4X12sX8
17. 4-4X12sX12
18. 4-4X14sX18
19. RAFTERS 4-4X12sX24
20. SKYLIGHT STEEL-FRAMED WIRED-GLASS
21. DOOR SLIDING GLASS

Foundation Floor

22. REINFORCED CONCRETE
23. EXPOSED AGGREGATE
24. RED BRICK OR QUARRY TILE

Materials

Top View of Typical Wall Construction

8'

candescent flood lamps are used as light for plants. One 150-watt floodlamp is all that is needed for a few plants, and three or four floodlamps would accommodate many plants in say, an area 8 X 10 feet. Standard incandescent lamps can be used in fixtures, but you might want to use special incandescent growth lamps; they incorporate both fluorescent and incandescent elements to furnish almost excellent light for plants. These are available under various trade names from manufacturers in your area.

Lamps, no matter which kind you use, should be placed at least 3 to 5 feet from the plant; this distance eliminates any chance of heat burning the foliage. Provide at least 12 to 14 hours of artificial light per day in the greenery. Install a special circuit and a timer switch to automatically turn lights on and off in case you forget.

The essentials for the indoor greenhouse are really simple: a floor that resists water stain, a lighting system and lamps, and of course, plants.

Another kind of greenhouse you might consider for a small indoor area is a tubular plastic and acrylic covered minigreenhouse with an arch shape. This is offered as a prefabricated kit and snaps together in fifteen minutes without a single nut, bolt, screw or tool required. It can occupy any space near a window in an office, home, or apartment, and can also be fitted with a clip-on "plant-lite". *(See list of suppliers at end of book).*

5 Advantages of a Greenhouse

In a greenhouse you can work with plants, enjoying nature first-hand. Your private Eden may be a place to grow cut flowers, sow seeds to get a head start on spring, or start vegetables *(and really save money)*. Also, and this is a big plus, you can relieve the day's tensions by working with nature.

Growing Plants from Seed

The gardener who grows his plants from seed gets more than economic advantages: he can have the most recently introduced plants. I still remember having the first dwarf red impatiens in full bloom long before they were available to the public. Also, by growing from seed you can have all the old favorites that are getting lost in the modern-day shuffle. A friend gave me some seeds of a forgotten iris, today unavailable commercially. From the seeds I have grown these flowers and in turn given seeds to other friends; this is an excellent way of keeping a line of plants going. Finally, often the color of flower or variety of vegetable you want is not available at your local garden center, so growing plants from seed in your greenhouse gives you a choice of selection.

Getting Started

You can buy seeds from suppliers or order from seed catalogs, everything from house plants to vegetables and herbs. Or you collect seeds from friends' plants or the roadside. After you have made your seed selections, get some seed starting mediums—vermiculite, sand, and so on—containers, and equipment. New growing mediums and containers are available at suppliers. Perlite is a good growing medium, and milled sphagnum moss represents a tremendous advance in seed-starting techniques. You can also use Jiffy peat pots or Poly-trays.

Seed Containers and Growing Mediums

There are many containers for starting seeds, both professionally made and homemade. Suppliers carry "starting kits," pots, plant mixes, and so forth. Just what kind of container you use depends upon your taste. For years my favorites have been the packing boxes *(flats)* for window glass because they are an ideal size, not too large or too small, and they are free. Flats range in size from 12 X 18 to 24 X 30 inches, 3 or 4 inches deep, and have drainage space between the boards. Flats are still available from glass dealers in some cities, usually free.

Other free containers to sow seeds in include such household items as coffee cans, aluminum and glass baking dishes, plastic cheese containers, and the aluminum pans that frozen rolls come in. Any household item you use as a container must be at least 3 inches deep and have some drainage facilities *(punch tiny holes in the bottom of pans)*. In aluminum and plastic containers the planting mix will dry out quickly, so water more frequently.

You can also use the standard clay pot for seed sowing. These excellent containers are inexpensive, always look neat, and hold enough moisture so that frequent watering is not necessary. Ask for azalea pans—squatty pots—now available in several sizes.

The growing medium you choose for seeds depends on what you want to grow. However, most seeds germinate easily in vermiculite or a standard "starting mix" *(at nurseries)*. I have found that a peat mix is good for cactus and succulents; standard vermiculite and milled sphagnum are very satisfactory for annuals and perennials; and for starting trees and shrubs I use equal parts of sphagnum and vermiculite. Good growing mediums are:

Milled sphagnum. This old-timer generally gives good results. Its disadvantage is that it has to be carefully watered to maintain an evenly moist bed.

Perlite. This is a light, clean, volcanic ash that does not absorb moisture readily, but it holds moisture within itself, providing a moist growing medium ideal for seeds. Mix in a little sterilized soil so seeds do not float to the top.

Vermiculite. Vermiculite is expanded mica that holds moisture a long time. It is sold under various trade names, and frequently it is packaged with added ingredients, which may or may not be a good idea *(I have not tried it yet).*

Many gardeners prefer a mixture of equal parts vermiculite, sphagnum, and perlite. Avoid packaged soil mixes because they are generally too heavy for successful seed sowing. But if nothing else is at hand, use it in combination with some sand.

Cut Flowers

When days are gray and your spirits are depressed, the best cure is to walk into your greenhouse and cut some flowers for indoor decoration. Growing blooms under glass is easy, convenient, and cheap with controlled conditions. For a continuous supply of flowers, place the plants directly in wooden benches filled with soil. Although carnations and chrysanthemums are always favorites for bench growing, snapdragons, asters, calendulas, and alyssum are also fine possibilities, and there are dozens more.

Prepare your soil bed with care; this and watering is almost all you have to do for splendid flowers. Fill the bench with a copius layer of drainage material—shards or pebbles. Now add a good potting soil; you want a rich soil to get plants to grow quickly. Next, put the seedlings in place. *(The seedlings can be plants you started yourself from seed in the greenhouse or seedlings you bought from a nursery.)* Do not water too much at first; keep the seedlings just barely moist. Keep the humidity at about 50 to 60 percent to encourage good growth. Try not to grow too many different kinds of plants at first. Try a few together, such as snapdragons and stock,

The advantages of your own greenhouse are many and one facet is starting your own plants from seed. What a saving! And what a satisfaction of growing your own. *(Photo by Matthew Barr).*

Seedlings grow under almost perfect conditions in a greenhouse and prosper to mature into healthy plants. There is a money saving here as well as the joy of working with living plants. *(Photo by Matthew Barr).*

the first year. The following year grow several kinds. In time you will gain actual know-how experience, and your home will have cut flowers year-round.

Because there are so many cut flowers for greenhouse growing, it is impossible to offer a comprehensive list. Here are some favorites to try:

Ageratum
Aster
Buddleia
Butterfly flower *(Schizanthus)*
Chrysanthemum
Delphinium
Marguerite
Marigold *(Tagetes)*
Nasturtium *(Tropaeolum)*
Pansy
Phlox *(annual)*
Snapdragon
Statice
Stock
Sweet pea
Zinnia

Starting Plants for Outdoors

As mentioned, besides being economical, growing plants in a greenhouse is an excellent way to stock the garden. You know what you have, and there is a great reward in looking over your landscape and knowing these are your plants. Start the seeds as described earlier in this chapter.

The following plants are ideal for starting in a greenhouse and getting a head start on spring:

Ageratum houstonianum
  (flossflower)
Anchusa capensis
Antirrhinum majus
  (snapdragon)
Arctotis stoechadifolia grandis
  (African daisy)
Calendula officinalis
  (pot marigold)

Centaurea cyanus
  (cornflower)
Cleome spinosa
  (spiderflower)
Cobaea scandens
  (cup-and-saucer vine)
Cosmos bipinnatis
Dimorphotheca aurantiaca
Gaillardia pulchella
  (annual)
Godetia grandiflora
Gypsophila elegans
  (annual)
Helichrysum bracteatum
  (strawflower)
Impatiens balsamina
  (balsam)
Linum grandiflorum
Lobelia erinus
  (annual)
Mathiola incana
  (stock)
Myosotis alpestris
Petunia hybrids
Pholx drummondii
  (annual phlox)
Reseda odorata
  (mignonette)
Salpiglossis sinuata
  (painted tongue)
Scabiosa atropurpurea
  (pincushion flower)
Tagetes erecta
  (African marigold)
T. patula
  (French marigold)
Thunbergia alata
  (black-eyed Susan)
Verbena hortensis
  (garden verbena)

Vegetables and Herbs

If you have the space, grow some vegetables and herbs in addition to plants. Your own vegetables are a fabulous bounty, especially during bleak winter days, and herbs for salads and stews—fresh from the greenhouse —are impossible to buy. It is not necessary to have a lot of vegetables, and space probably will prohibit it anyway, but a few carrots, beets, and tomatoes are always welcome.

The joys of vegetable growing far outweigh the care you have to give the plants. Most vegetables grown in greenhouses—tomatoes, radishes, carrots—need only a good lightweight, quick-draining soil and plenty of sun. Keep the plants well watered after the seedlings have been put in their permanent locations, and provide a buoyant humidity of about 50 percent.

Tomatoes can be grown in large tubs. In fact, there is now a tomato variety that was especially developed for container growing. Grow plants in 80F to a single stem and stake them for support or it will be impossible to handle them. Polinate blossoms by hand, or use a hormone-type tomato spray on the blossoms.

Bibb lettuce grow in the same temperature as tomatoes and need only an even soil and some sun. Carrots and beets need cooler growing conditions, about 45 to 55F.

You can start herbs from seeds or buy them as seedlings at nurseries; you may not want too many at first. A few selected herbs such as basil, dill, sweet marjoram, tarragon, and a few chives may be all you need for your cooking purposes. Most herbs do fine with plenty of sun and a minimum temperature of 50F. Use rich soil and provide near-perfect drainage. Provide adequate humidity and good air circulation, and mist the plants occasionally to keep them in tip-top condition.

In the main, this greenhouse is used for house plants and what fine specimens the plants are. Begonias and ferns, cacti and succulents, grace this home-made greenhouse. (*Photo by Matthew Barr*).

House Plants

Although it is true that house plants are for the house, it is nice to have these plants decorating the greenhouse if there is space. And there they will really grow, putting on a fine display. Indeed, medium-sized plants grown in the greenhouse will decorate your home and save you much money. With ideal conditions, plants will grow rapidly and soon be ready for indoor display.

If your house plants look a little wilted and need some help, move them to the greenhouse for a few months. The good humidity and light will help restore them to health and save you from replacing plants that may have perished in bad conditions indoors.

Most house plants will adapt and thrive in greenhouse conditions, that is, temperatures of 68 to 80F by day and 10 degrees less at night. Some tropical plants require high humidity and temperatures and so may not succeed in the greenhouse, but these plants are the exception rather than the rule.

Geraniums are the occupants of this greenhouse with nasturtiums growing at the door. Quite a pleasant sight. (*Photo by Matthew Barr*).

All kinds of plants thrive in this greenhouse including tuberous begonias, bouganvillea, seedlings, and even cut flowers. (*Photo by Clark Photo Graphics*). ▷

6 Greenhouse Conditions and Maintenance

Once you have built your greenhouse, you must consider such requirements as temperature, humidity, and ventilation. If the greenhouse is an all-glass, tightly enclosed room, these requirements are vital because glass is a poor conductor and greenhouses are invariably too hot in summer and too cold in winter. However, if you have avoided the all-glass unit, the problems of temperature, humidity, and ventilation are less stringent. Basically, conditions that approximate home conditions, that is, average temperatures of 70 to 80F during the day and some cooling at night, are fine. Humidity of 30 to 60 percent is ideal, along with year-round ciculation of air, which plants need.

Humidity

There is no reason to be confused about humidity in relation to growing plants. Average humidity *(30 to 50 percent)* is fine for most plants. High humidity, which is often recommended for plants by so-called experts, can do more harm than good in the winter because when coupled with dark days it can create a breeding ground for plant fungus and bacteria. Use an inexpensive hygrometer in the greenhouse to measure the moisture in the air. And remember that the more artificial heat you use in winter, the more moisture in the air will be necessary. On very hot days keep the humidity somewhat high. At night, humidity, like temperature, should be lower if you want good plant growth.

Usually, many plants growing together will create their own humidity, so expensive equipment *(misters, foggers)* is not necessary unless it is very hot. As long as you water routinely, there will be sufficient humidity in a room of plants to create good growth.

Temperature

Most plants do just fine with a temperature of 70 to 80F during the day and a 10- to 15-degree drop at night. You can maintain this temperature range in your own greenhouse without elaborate equipment; only in winter will you need to adjust heat for those very cold nights (and a few very cold nights will not harm plants). What will harm plants are sudden changes in temperatures, but by carefully manipulating windows and doors you can gradually cool summer evening temperatures. On very hot days, even the home greenhouse of wood and glass can get too hot for plants. When doors and windows are open, the sun can push the inside temperature past 100F, which dessicates plants and causes them to lose moisture fast. Spray and mist plants with water to keep them cool. Be especially alert in prolonged heat spells because you can lose many plants in a short few days if you do not cool them by misting or by providing outside shade *(see later section)*.

In winter, do not fret if the greenhouse is somewhat cool. It is far better to keep plants cool than too hot: they can recover from a chill but rarely from dehydration. On very windy and cold days, the temperature in a greenhouse can drop faster than you think, so make sure sufficient heat is provided. Again, avoid drastic temperature changes in the greenhouse.

Ventilation

I have always considered ventilation in my greenhouse more important than humidity or temperature because a good circulation of air is essential for all plants. Good ventilation provides relief from the sun, helps control such disease problems as mildew, and assures good humidity. When I first started growing orchids, I was always concerned with humidity and tropical heat, but in a few years I discovered that the plants did not object to coolness; indeed, they grew better as long as there was adequate ventilation.

The atmosphere in the greenhouse should be bouyant and fresh, never stagnant or stale. If you observe nature, you will note that few plants grow in stagnant places. Take a clue from Mother Nature: keep ventilation at a

VENTILATION, DRAINAGE

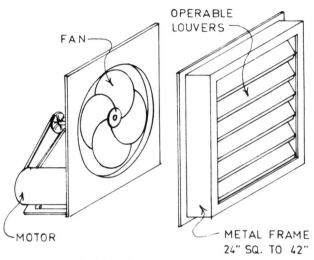

FAN

OPERABLE LOUVERS

MOTOR

METAL FRAME 24" SQ. TO 42"

Louvered Wall Fan

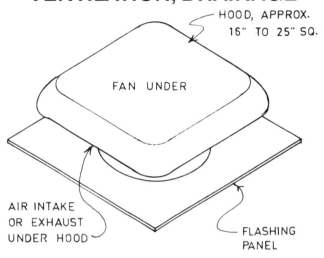

HOOD, APPROX. 16" TO 25" SQ.

FAN UNDER

AIR INTAKE OR EXHAUST UNDER HOOD

FLASHING PANEL

Roof Fan

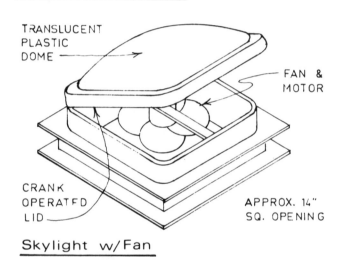

TRANSLUCENT PLASTIC DOME

FAN & MOTOR

CRANK OPERATED LID

APPROX. 14" SQ. OPENING

Skylight w/Fan

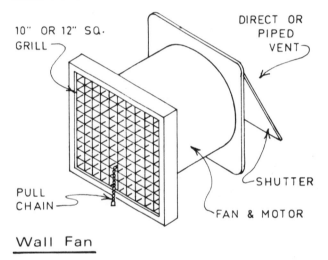

10" OR 12" SQ. GRILL

DIRECT OR PIPED VENT

PULL CHAIN

SHUTTER

FAN & MOTOR

Wall Fan

Ventilators

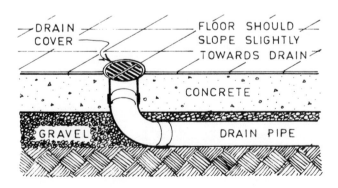

DRAIN COVER

FLOOR SHOULD SLOPE SLIGHTLY TOWARDS DRAIN

CONCRETE

GRAVEL

DRAIN PIPE

Solid Floor

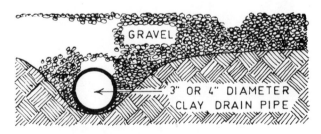

GROUND IS SLOPED TOWARDS CLAY PIPE IN TRENCH

GRAVEL

3" OR 4" DIAMETER CLAY DRAIN PIPE

Gravel Floor

maximum in your greenhouse. And even in winter be sure some air is entering the greenhouse. Remember that hot air rises, so provide some window facilities at the top of the greenhouse. When windows or vents are open, warm air flows out to cool the greenhouse and provides fresh air for best growing conditions.

Shading

Direct summer sun can heat up a greenhouse considerably and wreck havoc on plants. For example, some might die overnight if subject to even 1 day of extreme heat above 100F, and leaf temperatures over 120F immediately scorches and kills plant cells. In most parts of the country, unless your greenhouse is at an east exposure *(getting only morning sun),* you are going to have to provide some shading for the structure.

Old-fashioned paste or whiting powder can be applied with a spray or paintbrush, but this is a bother and ugly looking. Instead, use movable aluminum- or wood-slatted venitian blinds or bamboo rollups. They cost more than powders or paints, but they look better, are easy to install, and can be opened during periods of only bright light.

Plastic shading, like paint or powder, is also a bother and looks terrible. Use some nice curtains that break the sunlight yet allow some light through. Even better is special window trellage, which adds great charm to a building

(this is my preference, after trying other methods of shading).

Trellises can be built cheaply and installed with little effort; they will provide almost perfect light for plants as alternating shade and light is created.

Every greenhouse should have a hygrometer (shown center in this picture) to measure the amount of moisture in the air. It saves a lot of guesswork. *(Photo by Matthew Barr).*

Heating

Heating the greenhouse depends mainly where you live, the size of the greenhouse, and the design. Once greenhouse heating was a maze of pipes and problems, and only hot water heat was considered for plants. Today we know that many other types of heating are suitable. Installation and operation of the heating unit is not too difficult, but determining what kind of heating fuel to use—gas, oil, or electricity—can be tricky.

Before you select the heating system for your greenhouse, check local gas and electric rates. Decide which will be the most economical and then investigate specific systems. For my small greenhouse I used forced hot air heat by extending one duct from the house furnace. A professional installed the duct for $60. A small furnace with about three ducts *(for the average greenhouse)* would cost no more than $400.

The warm-air—gas-fired heater is popular for greenhouses; it has a safety pilot and thermostatic controls. You may have to provide masonry or metal chimneys so fumes are released outside. A nonvented heater does not need an outlet chimney; the combustible chamber is sealed and outside the greenhouse. The heater extends about 10 inches inside the greenhouse and needs only a 17-by 20-inch wall opening. Both types of heaters are approved by the American Gas Association (AGA) and are available through greenhouse dealers.

The warm-air—oil-fired heater is small, able to fit under a greenhouse bench. It will furnish sufficient heat for most average-sized greenhouses. It has a gun-type burner, a blower, a two-stage fuel pump, and full controls. This heater requires a masonry chimney or a metal smokestack above the roof.

Electric heaters are also satisfactory for small greenhouses. These units are automatic, built with a circulating fan, but heavy-duty electrical lines are necessary. The heater and thermostats should be installed by a professional in accordance with local electric codes.

See list of suppliers at end of book for greenhouse heaters.

Saving Heat

There are several ways to "store" heat in the greenhouses so you will not have to use so much fuel. These methods are relatively simple and involve using the right materials. For example, a concrete floor is a remarkable heat storer: it absorbs enough heat during the day *(if the structure faces south)* to keep the room warm a good part of the night, even in very cold climates. Masonry walls opposite the glass wall will also absorb the sun's heat and store it for night time radiation; even a wooden wall painted a dark color will help greatly to save on heating.

If you can afford it, use some thermopane, the insulating glass, in some areas of the greenhouse *(perhaps on the north wall, where winds are generally strongest)*. Thermopane can save as much as 30 percent heat in the area, and even though its initial installation is more expensive than standard glass, in the long run it certainly pays for itself *(see section on glass)*.

Once the greenhouse is built, landscape with hedges and shrubs at the sides where storms hit the hardest. This simple landscaping can effectively cut your heating bills a great deal, and planting some low-growing trees or shrubs in double rows at the corner of the greenhouse will add to the beauty of the total area. The natural barriers will also screen out dust, pollution, and noise.

Another effective way of cutting down on heat bills is to install heavy drapery; this thwarts cold drafts and keeps the greenhouse quite warm at night without extensively turning up the thermostat. Or better yet, use inexpensive wooden shutters or rollup blinds. These help keep out cold, thus cutting down on artificial heating.

Weatherstripping, sold in packages at hardware stores, can and should be used to further keep cold air out and warm air in the greenhouse. These effective products are especially easy to apply to wooden windows. They can cut heat loss by about 10 percent, so do not discount them as a gimmick. In Chicago, I always used them on greenhouse windows and cut my fuel bill quite a bit.

Insect Control

Even in the best managed greenhouse, some plants may be attacked by insects but there is no cause for alarm. If you catch insects before they have a foothold they are easy to eliminate. Thus, the main thing is to observe plants as you walk through the greenhouse; look for signs of insects. Most common plant insects are recognizeable on sight such

Temperature and hygrometer controls are located on the post in this place for plants. (*Photo by Matthew Barr*).

Ventilation is of prime importance in a greenhouse and here a fan is used. This in combination with the door provides ample circulation of air on very hot days. (*Photo by Matthew Barr*).

as aphids, mealy bugs, spider mites, scale, slugs, and snails. If you cannot identify the insect, pick if off the plant, kill it, and mail it in a plastic Baggie to your local County Agricultural Agency or Extension Service *(listed in phone book),* so they can identify it for you and tell you how to cope with it.

Aphids are pear-shaped small soft-bodied insects with a tiny beak that pierces plant leaves and extracts sap. Aphids may be black, red, brown, or gray, in color. Plants attacked by these insects lose vigor, may become stunted and leaves may curl or pucker.

Mealybugs have soft segmented bodies dressed in cotton wax. They often appear in leaf axils and take sap from plants and especially are fond of young growth.

Spider mites are difficult to see but they do spin webs which often gives them away. Foliage attacked by spider mites turns pale and may become stippled around the injured parts.

Scale are tiny and oval and have an armored shell or scales covering their body. They stay in one spot and extract sap from the plant. Leaf as well as stem damage may result when plants have scale.

Thrips are chewers and are very small slender insects with two pairs of long narrow wings. Thrips are usually indicated by silver sheen on the leaves.

Slugs and snails are easily recognizeable and no description is necessary; they are most apt to be found under pots and in dark corners of the greenhouse.

There are many preventatives for pests named above and these come in the forms of dusts, powders or sprays. Systemics—insecticides applied to soil—are also offered, and protect plants from some chewing and sucking insects for 6 to 8 weeks. Malathion will help control most of the insects mentioned above; for slugs and snails use a snail bait without methaldehyde which is highly poisonous. Snare-All is relatively safe if used as directed. With all chemicals, keep them out of reach of children and pets *(on a high shelf is good),* and always follow directions on the package to the letter.

If you object to using poisonous chemicals near and around the house *(and I do)* you can try some old-fashioned remedies. These ways are not as thorough as chemicals and take repeated applications but they are safe and avoid noxious odors.

1) Handpicking. Hardly pleasant but it can be done with a toothpick.

2) Soap and water. For many insects such as aphids and mealybugs, a solution of 1/2 pound of laundry soap (not detergent) and water works fine.

3) Alcohol. Alcohol on cotton swabs will effectively remove mealybugs and aphids from plants. Apply directly to insects.

4) Tobacco. Use a solution of old tobacco from cigarettes steeped in water for several days. Apply with cotton swab; gets rid of scale.

5) Water spray. May sound ineffective but works if used frequently and with strong enough force to wash away insects and their eggs.

6) Wipe leaves frequently. This simple step goes a long way to reduce insect problems in a greenhouse. It washes away eggs before they have a chance to hatch.

Maintenance

Any structure, including a greenhouse, needs periodic maintenance. If you check the greenhouse twice a year, you can remedy most problems with little effort or time. For example, foundations may develop cracks, but when caught in time they can be fixed by filling them in with appropriate compounds. If you are using glass for a covering, periodically check for broken panels and the glazing compound that holds the glass in place. If it is missing in a few places, replace it with more compound. In some cases complete reglazing with a new glazing compound may be best: if you have used putty instead of the newer glazing compounds, chances are it has become brittle with time and can be chipped away easily.

Repaint wooden members whenever it is needed. Do not neglect this because once excess moisture starts in wood it can cause havoc and travel quickly. If painting the inside of the greenhouse, clear out all plants rather than trying to do the job with plants intact; it is just too difficult, and paint fumes can harm plants.

Always check guttered and lipped grooves to be sure water is draining properly. Make any repairs immediately rather than waiting until a total replacement is necessary. Use a tar-based gutter paint for all gutters because it resists the extra moisture present in these areas.

The heater for this greenhouse is at far right deftly camouflaged with a vine on lattice work. (*Photo by Clark Photo Graphics*).

7 Greenhouse Accessories

Once your greenhouse is finished, you will need to determine where to put plants or, more importantly, what to put them on. Some large plants can be placed on the floor, but the majority will need benches or shelving *(putting plants directly onto the ground is currently out of style)*. Benches and shelving can be arranged in several different ways that will utilize the space more efficiently and still provide a pretty picture.

Commercial concrete or wooden benches are available, but they are bulky, not that attractive, and only come in certain sizes. Building your own benches and shelves is not that difficult, and you can create your own eye-pleasing designs and save some money.

Benches and Pedestals

The standard greenhouse bench is actually nothing more than a rectangular redwood planter supported by legs. The space under the bench is generally used for potted plants that need much shade. However, this arrangement is anything but handsome because there is a feeling of unbalance. If possible, add a decorative touch by enclosing the bottom with a panel of trellage; this allows light and air to circulate and yet looks good.

Do not make benches too long and never more than 36 inches wide. Remember, you want to be able to reach across with ease;

wider benches make getting to plants difficult. Long benches, say 6 feet, do not look as good as two small benches, and they are cumbersome.

You can plant directly into the benches: fill the bench with drainage material *(gravel or pot shards),* and then place soil to within 1 inch of the top of the planter. Or simply put in a bed

of white gravel and place potted plants on top for an attractive arrangement. Just what you are growing dictates how you use the benches. For example, if starting annuals and perennials, plant directly in the bench; for house plants, put potted plants in place.

To construct a bench, use redwood boards or slats spaced 1/4 inch apart to allow for water

Benches in tiers are always convenient for potted plants and look nice too. Benches of this kind make it easy to see and reach all plants, an important part of good greenhouse gardening. (*Photo by Matthew Barr*).

GREENHOUSE FURNISHINGS

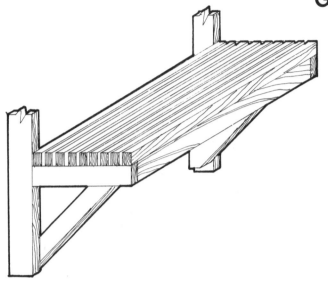

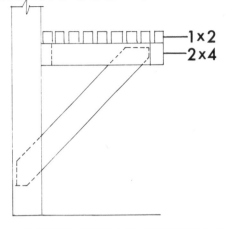

— 1×2
— 2×4

NOTE: USE ALL REDWOOD

Potting Tables

24"

30"

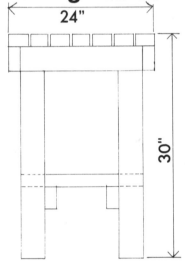

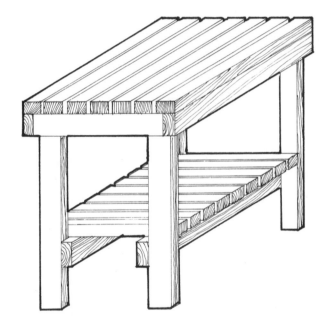

Portable Planter

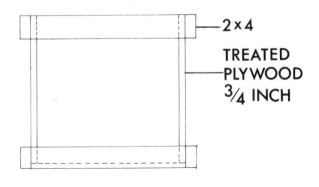

— 2×4

TREATED
PLYWOOD
¾ INCH

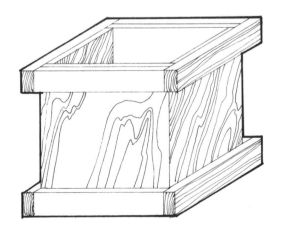

Slatted benches of redwood in this greenhouse are excellent because air is able to reach bottom of plant containers. Also, excess water spill is no problem. (*Photo by Matthew Barr*).

Pots can be suspended from ridges to hold plants to use ceiling space, or can also be set on shelves. (*Photo by Pat Matsumoto*).

drainage. The width of the bench should be 6 to 8 inches for ample planting space. Use wooden posts or galvanized pipes for supports. Do not put so many benches in the greenhouse that you do not have room to move around.

If you do not like benches, make plant pedestals and stands from redwood and place them in specific areas to create an eye-pleasing pattern. The pedestals can be of varying heights, from 24 to 48 inches, to provide a handsome setting for the plants *(use appropriately sized plants on the pedestals)*. Pedestals may assume many designs.

Hanging Devices

Plants in hanging containers are popular now and look good. They add a great deal of decorative beauty to the greenhouse and utilize otherwise wasted space. If you have a wooden frame structure, install eye bolts in the ceiling members and hang containers with chains, in macrame slings, or use commercial hangers. Special hangers are needed in the metal-framed greenhouse *(generally available from suppliers)*; attach them to ridge poles and roof bars. There is a wealth of plants for basket growing, and indeed, this is the only way to grow trailing plants to perfection. Set on benches or shelves, trailing plants do not have enough space to be shown to advantage.

Shelves

Shelves in your greenhouse can accommodate many plants and look handsome. Shelving can be redwood slats on L-shaped braces or more elaborate. I use 1 X 2 slats, 6 feet long, spaced 1/4 inch apart on heavy-duty galvanized L brackets, which is quite satisfactory. Five or six slats *(approximately 1 3/4 inches)* will give you space for some large pots too. Brace the slats every 3 feet.

Glass and acrylic shelves are also popular *(although more costly)*. Secure them with wood moldings at the edges for an easy installation. More elaborate shelf designs are possible too; we include some in the drawings. If you use shelving, try to prevent the foliage of the plants from touching the glass because this injures the leaves and would be harmful in cold weather. Leave 1 inch of space between the plant foliage and the glass of the greenhouse.

Closeup of simple bench construction; redwood is used throughout, treated, and makes a fine building material within a greenhouse. *(Photo by G. Burgess)*.

89

Photo by Clark Photo Graphics

Yearly Calendar for your Greenhouse

JANUARY

If you enjoyed your greenhouse during the summer and spring months, in January you will really realize why greenhouses are so desirable. In this gray, cold month, flowers at the windows are a joy, and a verdant greenery inside while all is bare outside lifts the spirits considerably. But although January is a month of beauty inside, it is also a month to do things in the greenhouse to have spring-flowering plants.

From late January on you can start Hyacinth, Daffodils, Crocus, Grape Hyacinths, and Snowdrops bulbs. Keep the plants in semi-shade until leaves are at least 4 to 5 inches tall; then bring them into bright light. You can also start caladiums and other tuberous plants and root cuttings of house plants.

Sow some perennial seed so you will have summer bloom. Try Cornflowers, Carkias, Impatiens, Larkspur, Marigolds, Petunias, Snapdragons, Statice, and Sweet Peas, and so on.

Water plants sparsely, especially on dark days; few plants die from not enough water in winter, but overwatering coupled with dark days can cause fungus to attack and kill them. Even though it is cold outside, be sure some fresh air gets into the greenhouse. Open windows slightly in midday; close them at night. Perhaps keep a small electric fan running to keep air circulating. Provide adequate artificial heat to keep temperature at 75F by day, 10 to 15 degrees lower at night. Do not let the house get too warm.

FEBRUARY

It may not look like spring outdoors, but in your greenhouse plants will already be awakening with new sprouts and shoots. This is the time to sow seed and increase watering somewhat and to be prepared for the upcoming sunnier days. Repot some plants *(the rest can wait until next month).*

Cineraria and Cyclamen should be available as florist plants now, and a few to perk up the greenhouse would be welcome. All kinds of tubers can be started, including Achimenes and Caladiums. Trim house plants and give them some fresh soil.

Provide adequate ventilation to maintain a healthy atmosphere, and also carefully protect plants against sudden February wind storms. Provide shutters or at least some burlap or some drapery at windows if you feel ambitious.

Seed to sow:
Candytuft
Cyclamen
Kalanchoe
Marigold
Primrose
Snapdragon
Sweet peas
Thunbergia

MARCH

This is a very busy month in the greenhouse. Now is the time to start seeds of annuals and perennials so plants will be ready for outdoors. Make sure the greenhouse has adequate circulation of air: not too cold, not too warm. Watch out for leaf burn on house plants such as African violets and ferns. Some shade protection might be necessary if you have an all-glass greenhouse.

Start vegetables for that basket bounty in summer. Get the seeds in or use prestart plants if they are available. Lettuce can be grown in hanging baskets and root crops started in deep planter boxes or tubs.

Do all kinds of cuttings now if you want to multiply your house plant stock, and increase your stock of Dahlias by dividing bulbs.

With the coming of warm weather insect eggs may start to hatch, so watch plants; if you see insects, eliminate them.

APRIL

April sun can be hot, so shading may now be necessary to protect plants from leaf burn. Be especially prudent about watering plants, and be sure soil is evenly moist. With good weather and warmth plants can use plenty of water. Many annual and perennial seeds and some vegetables can still be started. For tub growing try midget varieties such as eggplants, peppers, cucumbers, and tomatoes. Also grow some radishes and carrots for summer produce. Remember to give vegetables lots of sun and water. Do the rest of the re-potting of house plants and other

Photo by Pat Matsumoto

general chores such as trimming and pruning to prepare for the coming summer months.

Seeds to sow:
Anemone
Aster
Celosia
Freesia
Primrose
Snapdragon
Zinnia

MAY

Be sure plants have protection from the sun; ferns, palms, and orchids will all burn in direct sun. House plants can be revitalized easily in the good conditions of the greenhouse, and those already there will start rapid growth. Or you can move house plants into the house because they are in peak health. Increase watering and start a mild feeding program—there is ample light and sun now, so plants need that added boost of food.

Keep the greenhouse somewhat humid, and continue a regular watering and feeding program for most of your plants. Transfer vegetables outdoors or into large tubs if you want. Start some vines like Clematis and Morning glory to add more color to the greenery. Let them climb on walls and windows for a pleasant picture. There is still time to sow seeds of many annuals and perennials.

JUNE

This month the entire greenhouse assumes a lush look because everything is growing, and rapidly. You will want to spend more time with your plants as they thrive. It is a good idea to do some expert house cleaning and get the greenhouse really clean for sum-

mer before weather gets too warm. Inspect plants for insects and use appropriate preventatives if necessary.

Start seeds of tomatoes for a fall crop and some snapdragons for winter bloom. Water plants copiously and tend those vegetables and herbs *(this is the peak growing season)*.

Keep ventilation at an optimum, and settle back *(but not for too long)* and enjoy some summer color. Keep the greenhouse warm and humid to help plants grow quickly.

JULY

In July the main consideration is ample water because everything is growing. The sun is hot, the air is dry, and water is a must. Wet down greenhouse walks to increase humidity, which helps combat high temperatures. Keep air circulating in the greenhouse; open vents and windows so there is a soft flow of air. Mist plants with water to keep down heat, and again inspect plants for insects, which can cause trouble at this time. This is the month to start more seeds, such as:
Browalia
Calceolaria
Calendula
Lupine
Mignonette
Nemesia
Snapdragon
Stock
Sweet peas *(winter flowering)*
Wallflower

AUGUST

Although this month is hot, it can also bring some cool nights, so be prepared. Keep ventilation at the optimum, and eliminate any insects you might find. Keep feeding plants, but start tapering off on watering. This is the last time to pinch back such plants as chrysanthemums and carnations. Have the heating system checked to be sure it is in good working order for the fall and winter season.

Seed to start:
Blue lace flower
Browallia
Calceolaria
Calendula
Lupine
Marigold
Nasturtium
Pansy
Primrose
Snapdragon
Statice
Stock
Sweet peas
Thunbergia

SEPTEMBER

September usually brings cool nights and clear days, an ideal tonic for plants. The house may need some heat on some nights to provide warmth and to lower high humidity. To get the greenhouse ready for winter, trim and prune plants, and get house plants in order. Start resting bulbous plants like Gloxinias and Caladiums by putting them in their pots under benches. Discard plants that did not make it during the year. Do a last insecticide spraying to prevent insects and diseases.

Bulbs to start:
Brodiaea
Calla lily
Calochortus
Freesia
Hyacinth
Ixia
Montbretia
Narcissus

Ornithaogalum
Oxalis
Ranunculus
Sparaxis

OCTOBER

Pretty much follow September's schedule.

NOVEMBER

November is the time to sit back and enjoy the greenhouse; outdoors things may be slowing down and gray days may occasionally dot the month, but in the greenhouse it is still verdant and lovely. Cloudy weather is part of the month, which means you should taper off watering and feeding. Plants do not need any protection now, and what little sun there is will be welcome. Even though cold weather is on the way, be sure to provide adequate air circulation. Heat will probably be needed full time now but not so much that a stagnant, hot atmosphere is created.

Cuttings of various house plants, and flowering bulbs such as Amaryllis, Crinium, and Veltheimia can still be started.

DECEMBER

This is the season to enjoy your greenhouse, so do as little work as possible. Color should be splendid now (if you have prepared), and Poinsettias, crown of thorns, and Christmas cactus will be in full display. Browallias and Oxalis can also add to the color festival this month.

Keep most plants somewhat dry, without additional feeding; although it is cold outdoors, be sure to allow some ventilation in the greenhouse. Be on the alert for fungus disease, which can start

with cloudy days and cold weather, and if plants show signs of leaf mildew, apply appropriate remedies.

You can take branches of flowering plants like Japanese quince and cherry and Forsythia and force them. All they need is warm water to bear their lovely flowers.

Space all plants, walk through the greenery to appreciate nature and the season.

Photo by Clark Photo Graphics

94

List of Suppliers

Lumber is available from dealers in your area; I-beams, metal framing from building supply yards. All kinds of glass are at your local glass shops, and flexible and rigid plastic are at hardware stores and building supply houses.

Prefabricated greenhouses are available from dozens of manufacturers. These are the ones I have known through the years and have had correspondence with about their products. In addition to greenhouse kits, most of these companies also carry heaters, fans, and greenhouse accessories such as benches, tables and so forth.

Aluminum Greenhouse Inc.
14615 Lorain Avenue
Cleveland, Ohio 44111
Aluminum-and-glass greenhouses; supplies.

Gothic Arch Greenhouses
P.O. Box 1564
Mobile, Alabama 36601
Gothic arch design greenhouses; redwood-and-fiberglas construction. Supplies.

Environmental Dynamics
P.O. Box 996
Sunnymead, California 92388
Fiberglas and steel design; arches. Supplies.

Lord & Burnham
Irvington, N.Y. 10533
One of the largest manufacturers of aluminum-and-glass greenhouses.

Redwood Domes
P.O. Box 666
Aptos, California 95003
Redwood or metal domes of all types. Supplies.

Casaplanta
16129 Cohasset St.
Van Nuys, California 91406
Mini home greenhouses for apartment, office.

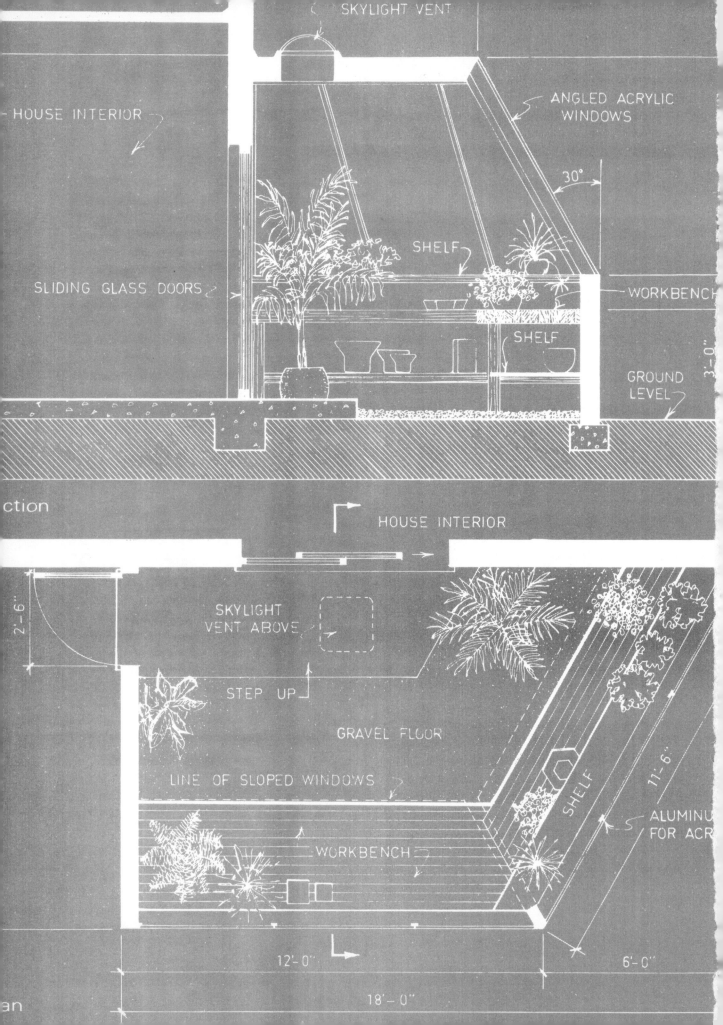

SKYLIGHT VENT

HOUSE INTERIOR

ANGLED ACRYLIC
WINDOWS

30°

SHELF

SLIDING GLASS DOORS

WORKBENCH

SHELF

GROUND
LEVEL

3'-0"

ction

HOUSE INTERIOR

2'-6"

SKYLIGHT
VENT ABOVE

STEP UP

GRAVEL FLOOR

11'-6"

LINE OF SLOPED WINDOWS

SHELF

WORKBENCH

ALUMINU
FOR ACR

12'-0"

6'-0"

an

18'-0"